THE COMPLETE CHEFMAN AIR FRYER COOKBOOK

Delicious and Simple Air Fryer Recipes for Beginners & Advanced

Seth Smerd

TABLE OF CONTENTS

INTRODUCTION

Air Frying Basics

In the simplest of terms, an air-fryer is a compact cylindrical countertop convection oven. It's a kitchen appliance that uses superheated air to cook foods, giving results very similar to deep-frying or high-temperature roasting. Many of us have convection ovens in our kitchens. In a standard oven, air is heated and the hot air cooks the food. In a convection oven, air is heated and then blown around by a fan. This creates more energy and consequently cooks foods faster and more evenly.

Air fryers use the same technology as convection ovens, but instead of blowing the air around a large rectangular box, it is blown around in a compact cylinder and the food sits in a perforated basket. This is much more efficient and creates an intense environment of heat from which the food cannot escape. The result is food with a crispy brown exterior and moist tender interior – results similar to deep-frying, but without all the oil and fat needed to deep-fry. In fact, when you are air-frying, you usually use no more than one tablespoon of oil!

Better still, an air fryer doesn't just cook foods that you would usually deep-fry. It can cook any foods that you would normally cook in your oven or microwave as well. It is a great tool for re-heating foods without making them rubbery, and is a perfect and quick way to prepare ingredients as well as make meals. To me, it is the best new kitchen appliance that has been introduced in recent years.

Is The Air Fryer Healthy?

The air fryer is not the only cooking method that cooks healthy food. The hype is in the fact that fried foods are very popular and obviously taste better than boiled foods.

Though Deep fried foods like fried chicken, French fries and the likes taste delicious, the draw back is the amount of oil needed to achieve that crispy delicious goodness we all love.

That's where the air fryer fills the gap. The air fryer makes fried foods healthier because it makes fried foods taste awesome with less oil. The method of cooking forcing hot air around the food in such a way that a little oil adds a level of delicious crispiness that can be compared with deep fried chicken. This crispy air fried chicken drumsticks is proof of the how the air fryer makes crispy chicken.

How To Clean An Air Fryer?

This machine allows you to enjoy your favorite fried foods guilt-free and with less fat and fewer calories. But even when you're using it, you're still 'frying' after, therefore it's essential to clean it after every use since grease or oil build-up can make your device smoke.

Most models come with dishwasher-safe parts, so make sure to check the manual before washing. Here is how you clean an air fryer:

1.First refer to your manual on how to clean your specific gadget. Some brands have dishwasher safe parts.

2.Unplug your fryer from the electric socket.

3.Remove basket, pans, racks or any insert that has been used. Wash them with hot soapy water. If there is any food or baked-on grease, keep these parts to soak in the hot soapy water for 5 - 10 minutes before scrubbing them with a non abrasive sponge.

4.Now take a non abrasive sponge or a damp cloth with a little bit of dish soap to wipe down the insides of your air fryer. Wipe the soap away using a clean damp cloth.

5.The next step is to turn the appliance upside down and start wiping the heating element using a damp cloth. If there is any hard residue on the main part, apply a paste of water and baking soda on the baked-on, and scrub it slowly using a soft-bristle scrub brush.

6.Wipe the foam away using a clean and dry cloth.

7.Now it's time to clean the exterior of your air fryer. Simply, wipe it down using a damp cloth with some soapy water and then wipe the soap away with a clean & dry cloth.

8.Set the removable parts on the counter to dry before reassembling.

This is how simple it is to clean an air fryer. It is important to clean an air fryer after every use to keep it in good condition, and help it last more.

Important Tips to Keep in Mind

1. Always have the grate in the basket. This allows hot air to circulate around the food, and also keeps the food from sitting in excess oil.

2. Air fryers are loud. When it's running, you'll hear whirring fans.

3. It's hands-on. Even browning requires you to remove the basket and shuffle the food around every few minutes.

4. It's fine to pull out the basket for a peek. You can do this at any point into the cooking process. No need to shut off the machine, as it shuts itself off when the basket is out.

5. Accordingly, make sure the drawer is pushed all the way in, or it won't turn back on. You'll know, because the air fryer will be suddenly quiet.

6. Food cooks fast, faster than you're used to! It's one of the best attributes of the air fryer. Your air fryer's manual likely has a handy table of cooking times and temperatures for common foods. The less food in the basket, the shorter the cook time will be; the more food, the longer it will be.

7. You may need a slightly lower temperature. A lot of air fryer recipes call for lower temperature settings than their conventional counterparts. This might seem fishy, but just go with it. Once again, air fryers get hot very fast and move that hot air around, so a slightly lower temperature will help keep food from getting too dark or crispy on the outside, while still being properly cooked on the inside.

POULTRY RECIPES

Tandoori Chicken Recipe

Servings: 4
Cooking Time: 15 minutes

Ingredients:
- 1 pound chicken tenders each cut in half
- ¼ cup Full-Fat Greek Yogurt
- 1 tablespoon Minced Ginger
- 1 tablespoon Minced Garlic
- ¼ cup Cilantro or sub parsley
- 1 teaspoon Kosher Salt
- ½ â€" 1 teaspoon Cayenne Pepper
- 1 teaspoon Turmeric
- 1 teaspoon Garam Masala
- 1 teaspoon Smoked Paprika to add a smoky flavor to the chicken, and color
- For Finishing
- 1 tablespoon Oil or ghee for basting
- 2 teaspoons Lemon Juice for finishing
- 2 tablespoons chopped cilantro for garnishing

Directions:
1. In a glass bowl, mix all ingredients except the basting oil, lemon juice and 2 tablespoons of cilantro. Marinate for 30 minutes.
2. Open up the air fryer and carefully lay the tandoori chicken in a single layer on either the rack or in the basket of your air fryer.
3. Using a silicone brush, baste the chicken with either oil or ghee on one side.
4. Cook at 350F for 10 minutes.
5. Remove and flip over the chicken, and baste on the other side,
6. Cook for another 5 minutes.
7. Using a meat thermometer, check to see if the internal temperature has reached 165F. Do not skip this step.
8. Remove and place on a serving plate. Add lemon juice and mix, and sprinkle with cilantro.

Huli Huli Chicken

Servings: 4
Cooking Time: 10 minutes

Ingredients:
- 4 Boneless Skinless Chicken Thighs
- For the sauce:
- 8 ounces canned pineapple chunks n juice, drained with juice reserved
- 1/4 cup Soy Sauce
- 1/4 cup Splenda or sugar
- 2 tbsp Ketchup
- 1 tbsp Minced Garlic
- 1 tbsp Minced Ginger
- 1/4 cup Chopped Green Scallions chopped

Directions:
1. Use a fork to poke holes into the chicken and place the chicken in a large bowl or in a Ziploc bag.
2. Make the sauce.
3. Remove 1/4 cup of juice from the canned pineapple and drink the rest as your reward. Set aside the pineapple chunks.
4. In a small microwave safe bowl, mix together 1/4 cup of pineapple juice, soy sauce, sugar, ketchup, ginger and garlic.
5. Pour half the sauce over the chicken Mix until the thighs are well-coated with the marinade. Reserve the rest of the sauce to cook as a dipping sauce (below).
6. Set aside the chicken to marinate for 30 minutes or up to 24 hours in the refrigerator.
7. Place the marinated chicken in the airfryer at 360F for 15 minutes, turning half way through.
8. Meanwhile, place the reserved sauce in the microwave and cook on high for 45-60 seconds, stirring every 15 seconds. You are going to cook this until you get a thick glaze or pouring sauce that you can use with the cooked chicken
9. Using a meat thermometer, ensure your chicken has reached an internal temperature of 165F.
10. Remove chicken to a serving tray, garnish with pineapples and green onions and serve with the thickened sauce poured over all of it.

Air Fryer Chicken

Servings: 4
Cooking Time: 15 minutes

Ingredients:
- For the Chicken Fry
- 1 pound Boneless Skinless Chicken Thighs each thigh cut into 3 pieces
- 1 large Onion cut into 1.5 inch thick slices
- 1 tablespoon Coconut Oil
- 2 teaspoons Minced Ginger

- 2 teaspoons Minced Garlic
- 1 teaspoons Smoked Paprika
- 1 teaspoons ground fennel seeds
- 1 teaspoons Garam Masala
- 1 teaspoon Turmeric
- 1 teaspoon Kosher Salt
- 1/2-1 teaspoon Cayenne Pepper
- Vegetable Oil for spraying the chicken while cooking
- For Finishing
- 2 teaspoons Lemon Juice
- 1/4 cup Chopped Cilantro or Parsley

Directions:

1. Make the Chicken Fry: Using a fork, pierce the chicken well all over to allow the marinade to penetrate.
2. In a large bowl, mix together all ingredients and allow the chicken to marinate for at least 30 minutes, or up to 24 hours.
3. Place chicken and vegetables into the air fryer basket. Spray the chicken and onion with some vegetable oil.
4. Set your air fryer to 360F for 15 minutes. Half way through, remove the basket, spray the chicken with more vegetable oil, and shake it about.
5. At the end of the cook time, use a meat thermometer, ensure your chicken has reached an internal temperature of 165F.
6. Remove the chicken and vegetables to a serving tray.
7. Sprinkle with fresh lemon juice and cilantro and serve.

Pecan Crusted Chicken

Servings: 4
Cooking Time: 12 minutes

Ingredients:
- 1 pound chicken tenders
- 1 teaspoon Kosher Salt
- 1 teaspoon Ground Black Pepper
- 1/2 teaspoon Smoked Paprika
- 1/4 cup Coarse-Ground Mustard
- 2 tablespoons Sugar-Free Maple Syrup or honey
- 1 cup finely-crushed pecans

Directions:
1. Place the chicken tenders in a large bowl.
2. Add salt, pepper and smoked paprika and mix well until the chicken is coated with the spices.

3. Pour in honey and mustard and mix well.
4. Place the finely-crushed pecans on a plate.
5. Working with one chicken tender at a time, roll the tenders into the crushed pecans until both sides are coated. Brush off any excess.
6. Place the tenders into the air fryer basket and continue until all tenders are coated and in the air fryer basket.
7. Set the air fryer to 350F for 12 minutes until the chicken is cooked through and the pecans are golden brown before serving.

Air Fryer Peanut Chicken

Servings: 4
Cooking Time: 20 minutes

Ingredients:
- 1 pound Bone-in Skin-on Chicken Thighs
- For the Sauce
- 1/4 cup Creamy Peanut Butter
- 1 tablespoon Sriracha Sauce (adjust for your spice needs)
- 1 tablespoon Soy Sauce
- 2 tablespoons Thai sweet chili sauce
- 2 tablespoons lime juice
- 1 teaspoon Minced Garlic
- 1 teaspoon Minced Ginger
- 1/2 teaspoon Kosher Salt to taste
- 1/2 cup hot water
- For the Garnish
- 5-6 teaspoons Cilantro finely chopped
- 1/4 cup Chopped Green Scallions
- 2-3 tablespoons crushed peanuts

Directions:
1. Mix together peanut butter, sriracha, soy sauce, sweet chili sauce, lime juice, and salt. Pour in the hot water and mix until you have a smooth mixture.
2. Place the chicken in a zip-top bag. Pour in half of the sauce and mix until the chicken is well coated. If you have the time, allow the chicken to marinate for 30 minutes or up to 24 hours in the refrigerator.
3. Remove the chicken from the bag, bringing with it as much of the marinade as you can. Place the coated chicken in the air fryer basket.
4. Set the air fryer to 350F for 20-22 minutes or until the chicken thighs are heated 165F at their thickest part.
5. Garnish with cilantro, onion, and peanuts. Serve with the rest of the sauce for dipping.

Keto Buffalo Chicken Dip

Servings: 4

Cooking Time: 15 minutes

Ingredients:

- 4 cups Rotisserie Chicken shredded
- 1/2 cup Onion chopped
- 1/4 cup Cream
- 1/4 cup hot wing sauce
- 1/4 cup blue cheese crumbled
- 2 ounces Cream Cheese diced
- pepper
- 1/4 cup Chopped Green Scallions chopped

Directions:

1. Preheat oven to 350F. Spray an 8 x 8 baking dish.
2. Mix together chicken, onion, hot wing sauce, cream, diced cream cheese, blue cheese, salt, and pepper.
3. Bake at 400F for 15 minutes. Remove from the oven and stir well to mix the cheeses. Cover with foil and let it rest for 2-3 minutes.
4. Garnish with chopped green onions and serve.

Air Fryer Turkey Breast

Servings: 4

Cooking Time: 40 minutes

Ingredients:

- 1 2 pound turkey breast
- 1/4 cup olive oil
- 2 tsp Fresh Sage diced
- 2 tsp Rosemary diced
- 2 tsp Kosher Salt
- 1 tsp Fresh Thyme diced
- 2 tbsp truvia brown sugar

Directions:

1. In a mixing bowl, whisk together the Olive Oil, spices, and sweetener to create a tasty coating
2. On a large plate or platter, massage the olive oil and spice blend into the turkey breast. Ensure you get the oil on top of and below the turkey breast skin for proper crisping
3. Add the seasoned turkey breast to your air fryer at 350 and cook for 20-25 minutes

4. Once the first cooking cycle is complete, flip the turkey breast and cook for an additional 20-25 minutes.
5. Place the cooked turkey breast inside of a tinfoil "tent" to rest for an additional 10 minutes.
6. Check the internal temperature with a meat thermometer. Once it reaches 165F, you are safe to slice and serve.

Air Fryer Chicken Nuggets

Servings: 6
Cooking Time: 10 minutes

Ingredients:
- 1 pound ground chicken
- 1 egg
- 1 cup flour
- 1 cup panko breadcrumbs
- 1 tsp kosher salt
- 1 tsp black pepper
- 1 tsp garlic powder

Directions:
1. In a large bowl, mix the ground chicken with the eggs.
2. In a separate bowl mix together the flour, bread crumbs, and spices.
3. Preheat your air fryer to 400F
4. Spray the outside coating of the formed chicken nuggets with cooking spray
5. Carefully place the oil coated ground chicken nuggets in the air fryer basket.
6. Cook for 8-10 minutes, flipping half way through the cooking time.

Air Fryer Breaded Chicken Wings

Servings: 4
Cooking Time: 20 minutes

Ingredients:
- 1 pound chicken wings
- 3 tablespoons Vegetable Oil
- 1/2 cup All-Purpose Flour
- 1/2 teaspoon Smoked Paprika
- 1/2 teaspoon Garlic Powder
- 1/2 teaspoon Kosher Salt
- 1/2 teaspoon freshly crushed peppercorn

Directions:

1. Place chicken wings in a large bowl. Pour in the oil and then toss to coat the wings well.
2. In a separate bowl, add dry ingredients and whisk until combined.
3. One at a time, place oiled wings in the dry mixture and coat with breading, then place each wing on in the air fryer basket.
4. Set your airfryer to 400F and cook for 20 minutes flipping half way through.
5. Use a meat thermometer to ensure the chicken wings have reached an internal temperature of 165F, and the breading is brown and crunchy before serving.

Air Fryer Chicken Tenders

Servings: 4
Cooking Time: 15 minutes

Ingredients:
- 1 pound chicken tenderloins
- 1 Eggs
- 1/2 cup Superfine Almond Flour
- 1/2 cup powdered Parmesan cheese (the cheap stuff in the green can)
- 1/2 teaspoon Kosher Salt
- 1 teaspoon pepper
- 1/2 teaspoon Cajun seasoning or cayenne, or chili powder

Directions:
1. In a small, relatively flat bowl, beat the egg.
2. In a ziptop bag, mix the almond flour, cheese, salt, pepper, and seasoning.
3. Get a paper plate or dinner plate ready.
4. Spray your air fryer basket with oil.
5. Dip each tender in the egg and place on the plate until all the tenders have been dipped. Don't try to dip it in the breading or else you'll have messy hands and clumps in the breading. Just line up the eggy tenders until they're all ready.
6. Now use a fork to pick up one tender at a time. Put that in the zip top bag and shake that bag like you mean it. Ensure the tenders are well covered in the almond mixture.
7. Do NOT dip in egg and breading again. Tried it. Hugely messy and less tasty.
8. Use the fork to pull out that tender and place it in your air fryer basket.
9. Spray the tenders with oil.
10. Cook at 350F for 12 minutes or until the inside registers 160F. Raise temperature to 400F for 3 minutes to brown the crust.
11. Serve with Big Mac sauce.

Cilantro Pesto Chicken Legs

Servings: 2
Cooking Time: 20 minutes

Ingredients:
- 4 chicken drumsticks
- 1/2 cup Cilantro
- 1/2 Jalapeño Peppers
- 8 cloves Garlic
- 2 thin slices Ginger
- 2 tablespoons Oil
- 2 tablespoons Lemon Juice
- 1 teaspoon Kosher Salt

Directions:
1. Place drumsticks in a flat tray. Using the tip of a sharp knife, score small slashes into the chicken at regular intervals so that the marinade can penetrate the chicken.
2. Finely chop the cilantro, pepper, garlic and ginger and place in a small bowl.
3. Add salt, oil and lemon juice to the chopped vegetables and mix well.
4. Spread this mixture over the chicken. Overcome any inhibitions you may have about touching raw chicken and lovingly massage the marinade into the chicken.
5. Let the chicken marinate for 30 minutes or up to 24 hours in the refrigerator.
6. When you are ready to cook, place the chicken legs into the air fryer basket, skin side up.
7. Set your airfryer to 390F for 20 minutes for meaty chicken legs. Halfway through, flip the chicken legs over.
8. Use a meat thermometer to ensure that the chicken has reached an internal temperature of 1650F. Remove and serve with plenty of napkins.

Turkish Chicken Kebab Recipe

Servings: 4
Cooking Time: 15 minutes

Ingredients:
- 1/4 cup Full-Fat Greek Yogurt
- 1 tbsp Minced Garlic
- 1 tbsp Tomato Paste
- 1 tbsp Vegetable Oil
- 1 tbsp Lemon Juice
- 1 tsp Kosher Salt

- 1 tsp Ground Cumin
- 1 tsp Smoked Paprika
- 1/2 tsp Ground Cinnamon
- 1/2 tsp Ground Black Pepper
- 1/2 tsp Cayenne Pepper
- 1 lb Boneless Skinless Chicken Thighs each cut into 4 pieces

Directions:

1. In a large bowl, stir together the Greek yogurt, garlic, tomato paste, lemon juice, oil, salt, cumin, paprika, cinnamon, black pepper, and cayenne pepper until the spices are well-blended into the yogurt.
2. Add the chicken pieces and mix until the chicken is well-coated with the marinade. Allow the chicken to marinate for 30 minutes or for up to 24 hours in the refrigerator.
3. Remove the chicken from the marinade and place in a single layer in the air fryer basket. Set the air fryer to 370°F and cook the chicken for 10 minutes.
4. Open the air fryer and flip over the chicken. Set the air fryer to 370°F and cook the chicken for another 5 minutes.
5. Test with a meat thermometer to ensure the chicken has reached an internal temperature of 165°F before serving.

Air Fried Chicken Shawarma

Servings: 4
Cooking Time: 15 minutes

Ingredients:
- For the Shawarma Spice
- 2 teaspoons Dried Oregano
- 1 teaspoon Ground Cinnamon
- 1/2 teaspoon Ground Allspice
- 1/2 teaspoon ground cayenne pepper
- 1 teaspoon Ground Cumin
- 1 teaspoon Ground Coriander
- 1 teaspoon Kosher Salt
- For the Chicken
- 1 pound Boneless Skinless Chicken Thighs cut into large bite-size chunks
- 2 tablespoons Vegetable Oil
- For Serving
- Tzatziki (greek yogurt-cucumber dip)
- Pita Bread

Directions:

1. For the shawarma spice: In a small bowl combine oregano, cinnamon, allspice, cayenne, cumin, coriander,

and salt.

2. For the chicken: In a large bowl combine chicken, oil, and shawarma spice mix; toss to coat. Allow to stand for 30 minutes at room temperature or cover and chill up to 24 hours in the refrigerator.

3. Place chicken in the air fryer basket. Set air fryer to 350°F for 15 minutes.

4. At the end of cook time, use a meat thermometer to ensure chicken has reached an internal temperature of 165°F.

5. For serving: Transfer chicken to a serving platter. Serve with tzatziki and pita bread.

Bacon Wrapped Stuffed Chicken

Servings: 4
Cooking Time: 15 minutes

Ingredients:
- 2 large chicken breasts butterflied and pounded thin to about 1/2 inch thickness
- 1/2 cup Frozen Spinach thawed & drained
- 1/4 cup Cream Cheese room temperature
- 1/4 cup shredded Parmesan cheese
- 2 tablespoons Jalapeño Peppers chopped
- 1 teaspoon Ground Black Pepper
- 1/2 teaspoon Kosher Salt
- 6 slices Bacon
- 4 teaspoons Cajun Seasoning

Directions:
1. In a small bowl, mix together spinach, cream cheese, Parmesan cheese, jalapenos, salt and pepper.

2. Place the butterflied chicken breasts on a flat surface. Spread the cream cheese mixture evenly across the two breasts.

3. Starting with the narrow end, roll up the chicken breast, ensuring the filling stays inside.

4. Dust each of the breasts with Cajun seasoning, patting it in to ensure it sticks to the chicken breast.

5. Wrap each chicken breast in 3 slices of bacon each. Place the wrapped chicken breasts in the air fryer basket.

6. Set fryer to 350°F for 30 minutes. Use a meat thermometer to ensure the chicken has reached an internal temperature of 165F.

Herb Roast Chicken

Servings: 4
Cooking Time: 25 minutes

Ingredients:

- 2 tablespoons salted butter or ghee softened
- 1/2 teaspoon Kosher Salt
- 1/2 teaspoon Smoked Paprika
- 1/2 teaspoon Dried Thyme
- 1/4 teaspoon dried rosemary
- 1/4 teaspoon Garlic Powder
- 1/4 teaspoon Ground Black Pepper
- lemon wedges for serving
- 2 bone-in, skin-on chicken breast halves about 10 ounces each

Directions:

1. In a small bowl combine butter, salt, paprika, thyme, rosemary, garlic powder, and black pepper. Stir until thoroughly combined.
2. Using a small sharp knife, carefully loosen the skin on each breast half, starting at the thin end of each half. Very carefully separate the skin from flesh, leaving skin attached at thick end of each breast. Divide herb butter into quarters. Rub one-quarter of the butter onto the flesh of each breast. Fold and lightly press skin back onto each breast. Rub remaining butter onto skin of each breast.
3. Place chicken in air fryer basket. Set fryer to 375°F for 25 minutes. At end of cook time, use a meat thermometer to ensure the chicken has reached an internal temperature of 165°F.
4. Let chicken rest for 5 to 10 minutes. Serve with lemon wedges.

Low Carb Chicken Shawarma

Servings: 4
Cooking Time: 10 minutes

Ingredients:

- 1 pound Boneless Skinless Chicken Thighs or breasts, cut into large, bite-size chunks (if using bone-in, increase time by 1-2 minutes)
- 1 teaspoon olive oil to marinate
- 2 teaspoons Oil to brown chicken
- 1 cup Onion thinly sliced
- 1/4 cup Water
- Shwarma Spice (Double batch)
- 2 teaspoons Dried Oregano
- 1 teaspoon Ground Cinnamon
- 1/2 teaspoon Ground Allspice
- 1/2 teaspoon Cayenne Pepper
- 1 teaspoon Ground Cumin
- 1 teaspoon Ground Coriander
- 1-2 teaspoons Kosher Salt

Directions:

1. Place the cut up chicken in a ziplock bag, pour in the olive oil, and pour in half the spice mix. Save the other half of the spice for the next time you make this recipe.

2. Smoosh it all up together so that the chicken is evenly coated in the oil and spices.

3. At this point, you could freeze it for later cooking, or you could leave it in the fridge to marinate for as long as you have. I'd make one batch now and freeze one.

4. When you're ready to cook it, heat the Instant Pot on sauté and when it's hot, add the chicken in a single layer. Let it sear for a few minutes and then flip over.

5. Add the onions in there. Traditionally, it's not cooked with onions, but we need something to add flavor to the broth and the chicken, and onions not only add flavor, but they also release a little water so it means you've got to add less plain water to the Instant Pot.

6. Pour in the 1/4 c of water, deglaze the pan if needed, and cook at high pressure for 10 minutes, using QPR

7. Remove chicken and cut into smaller bites but don't shred.

8. Enjoy with https://twosleevers.com/greek-tzatziki-yogurt-cucumbers/tzatziki for a tasty, low-carb dinner.

9. Oven or Air Fryer directions

10. Heat oven to 350F and line a baking pan with foil, or line your air fryer basket with foil

11. Spray or pour just a little extra oil to crisp the chicken a little during baking

12. Cook in oven for 10-15 minutes turning once. Test for doneness.

13. Cook in air-fryer for 10 minutes, turning once. Test for doneness.

Low Carb Indian Chicken Tikka Bites

Servings: 4

Cooking Time: 10 minutes

Ingredients:

- 1 pounds chicken thighs or breast, boneless skinless, cut into bite size cubes
- 1/2 cup Full-Fat Greek Yogurt
- 3-4 cloves Minced Garlic minced
- 2 teaspoons Minced Ginger minced
- 1/4 cup Cilantro chopped
- 1 teaspoon Kosher Salt
- 1 teaspoon Garam Masala
- 1/2 teaspoons Turmeric
- 1/2 teaspoons Ground Cumin
- 1/2 teaspoons Ground Coriander
- 1/2 teaspoons Smoked Paprika
- 1/4 teaspoons Cayenne Pepper
- 2 tablespoon Ghee

- 1 Lemon juiced

Directions:

1. Mix together chicken, yogurt, garlic, ginger, cilantro, salt, garam masala, cayenne, cumin, coriander, paprika, and let the chicken marinate for an hour or up to 24 hours. If you're using chicken breast, give it at least an hour for the yogurt to marinate the chicken

2. When you're ready to cook this, heat a skillet, and when it's hot, add two tablespoons of ghee. You want a skillet that's large enough to let your chicken rest in a single layer across the pan, or be ready to cook it in batches. You want to quick cook this at high heat, frying in the ghee, not braise this.

3. Carefully place the chicken in the skillet, and after 3-4 minutes, using tongs, turn the pieces to sear the other side. Once both sides are seared, you can reduce the heat a little to finish cooking the pieces, but all in all, you're looking at about 10 mins at most in the skillet, especially if you cut into bite-sized pieces as instructed

4. Spritz the lemon juice across all the chicken right before serving.

5. Air fryer

6. If you're trying to avoid fat, you can cook this in an air-fryer at 400F for 12 minutes, turning half way through. They're a little dryer than the skillet method but the meat is still tender due to the yogurt marinade.

7. Spritz the lemon juice across all the chicken right before serving.

Chicken Coconut Meatballs

Servings: 4
Cooking Time: 15 minutes

Ingredients:
- 1 pound Ground Chicken
- 2 Chopped Green Scallions finely chopped
- 1/2 cup Cilantro chopped
- 1 tablespoon Hoisin Sauce
- 1 tablespoon Soy Sauce
- 1 teaspoon Sriracha Sauce
- 1 teaspoon Sesame Oil
- 1/4 cup Unsweetened Shredded Coconut
- Kosher Salt to taste
- Ground Black Pepper to taste

Directions:

1. Heat oven to 350F.

2. Mix all ingredients together gently. It makes a wet and sticky mixture.

3. Line a cookie sheet with foil . Using a small scoop or a teaspoon, drop rounds of the mixture onto the foil-lined cookie sheet.

4. Bake until they reach an internal temperature of 150-160F, about 15-20 minutes.
5. Move sheet close to broiler and broil for a few minutes to brown the tops if you like.
6. Airfryer
7. These turned out really nice in an airfryer, the only problem is i could only fit 6-8 at a time and you'd have to do it in batches.
8. Cook at 350F for 10 minutes, flipping once, until they reach an internal temperature of 150-165F.
9. Brown at 400 for 2-3 minutes.

Thai Yellow Curry Baked Chicken Thighs

Servings: 4
Cooking Time: 25 minutes

Ingredients:
- 1 pound Boneless Skinless Chicken Thighs
- 2 tablespoons Thai yellow curry paste
- 1/2 cup Full-Fat Coconut Milk
- 3 cloves Garlic
- 2 teaspoons Minced Ginger
- 1/8 cup crushed peanuts for topping (optional)

Directions:
1. n a quart ziplock bag put in the chicken, followed by all the other ingredients.
2. Zip the top of the bag securely and then start smooshing all the ingredients together until well mixed.
3. Let the bag rest overnight or at least an hour to let the flavors meld.
4. Heat oven to 425 degrees. Put the chicken and the sauce in a pie pan.
5. Cook for 20 minutes or until internal temperature reaches 165 degrees.
6. I served this with roasted cauliflower that I cooked at the same time, and in a separate pan I also made Indian-style Chicken thighs so that I had two different flavors of chicken to serve.

Crispy Air Fryer Chicken Parmesan

Servings: 4
Cooking Time: X minutes

Ingredients:
- 2 chicken breasts roughly 1 lb
- 2 tablespoons all purpose flour almond and GF flour may also work
- 1 egg beaten
- ½ cup Panko breadcrumbs
- ¼ cup parmesan cheese freshly shredded

- 1 teaspoon dried oregano
- ½ teaspoon salt
- ½ cup marinara sauce
- ¼ cup mozzarella cheese shredded
- To serve
- fresh basil leaves torn

Directions:

1. Prepare chicken- Slice chicken in half horizontally to create two thin halves. Watch the video above if you are wondering how to do this.
2. Breading the chicken- Arrange three shallow bowls. In the first bowl, add the flour. In the second bowl, beat the eggs. In the third bowl, stir together the Panko, oregano, parmesan cheese and salt.
3. Working in batches, coat the chicken breast in flour (1), tapping so excess falls off. Next, dredge in the beaten eggs (2) until well coated. Allow excess egg to drip off. Finally, press both sides in the panko mixture (3), flipping until it is completely coated.
4. Transfer to a clean plate, and repeat with remaining chicken slices.
5. Cook- Preheat the air fryer to 400°F for at least five minutes. Arrange breaded chicken in the air fryer, and cook for 10 minutes, flipping halfway.
6. Check to ensure your chicken has reached 165°F (or very close to it) using an instant read thermometer.
7. Adding the marinara- Once chicken has reached 165°F internally, spoon 2 tablespoons of marinara on the top of each chicken breast. Sprinkled with shredded mozzarella, pressing into the marinara so it doesn't blow around in the air fryer.
8. Return to the air fryer for another 1- 2 minutes, until cheese has fully melted.
9. Serve- Sprinkle with fresh basil leaves, and enjoy.

NOTES

Storage & reheating

Chicken parmesan is best served fresh, as the breading loses it's crispy texture as it is stored. With that being said, it's safe to store and reheat:

if you plan to reheat later, do not add marinara and mozzarella

store in an air tight container for up to 4 days

heat air fryer to 350°F

add chicken and cook for 3-5 minutes, adding the marinara and mozzarella during the last 2 minutes of cook time

Air Fryer Chicken Fajitas

Servings: 4
Cooking Time: 10 minutes

Ingredients:

- 1 lb chicken breasts sliced into ¼ inch thick strips

- 2 bell peppers sliced into strips
- 1 red onion sliced into strips
- 1 tablespoon olive oil
- 1 tablespoon sugar
- ¾ teaspoon salt
- 1 tablespoon chili powder
- 1.5 teaspoon cumin
- 1.5 teaspoon paprika
- ½ teaspoon garlic powder
- ½ teaspoon onion powder
- ⅛-1/4 teaspoon cayenne optional
- To serve
- lime juice
- tortillas
- cilantro
- sour cream
- avocado

Directions:

1. Heat air fryer to 400°F or 200°C.
2. Mix together ingredients- In a large bowl, mix together the chicken, bell peppers, onion and olive oil until evenly coated.
3. Add all spices: sugar, salt, chili powder, cumin, paprika, garlic powder, onion powder and cayenne. Mix until chicken and vegetables are evenly seasoned.
4. Arrange in the air fryer:
5. Oven-style- spread evenly on the tray(s), making sure they are in a single layer. It's OK if the ingredients touch but you don't want multiple layers.
6. Basket-style- you may need to work in multiple batches. Add in a single layer to the basket.
7. Cooking- Cook for 5 minutes, then use tongs to flip and separate the chicken. If using an air fryer with trays, rotate the trays. Cook for another 3-5 minutes.
8. When chicken is cooked through and bell peppers are slightly softened, remove and serve with suggested toppings.

NOTES

Storage

After cooling completely, portion out into a meal prep container. Refrigerate for up to 4 days.

Reheating

Heat the air fryer to 350°F. Add fajita filling to the basket or arrange on trays, then heat for 5 minutes, or until warmed through.

Air Fryer Whole Chicken

Servings: 6
Cooking Time: 45 minutes

Ingredients:
- 2 teaspoons onion powder
- 2 teaspoons garlic powder
- 1 teaspoon salt
- 1 teaspoon pepper
- 1 teaspoon paprika
- 1 tablespoon olive oil
- 3 lb whole chicken

Directions:
1. Spice rub- in a small bowl, mix together the onion powder, garlic powder, salt, pepper and paprika. Add in the olive oil, and stir until it forms a paste.
2. Prepare chicken- use a spoon to loosen the breast skin of the chicken. Add ⅓ of the rub under the skin of the chicken, using your hands or the spoon to disperse it evenly. Rub the remainder of the paste all over the chicken, coating the breast, thighs, wings and back.
3. Cook- Heat the air fryer to 350°F for at least 5 minutes. Add the chicken, and cook breast side down for 40 minutes.
4. Flip the chicken- After 40 minutes, carefully dump the chicken breast side up onto a cutting board, then use spatulas to carefully transfer it back into the air fryer breast side up. Cook for 7-10 minutes breast side up, until skin is golden.
5. Rest chicken- allow chicken to rest on a cutting board for at least 10 minutes before carving.

NOTES

Storage

Cool completely, then store in an air tight container in the fridge for up to 4 days, or in the freezer for up to 3 months.

Reheating

Reheat in a frying pan, using tongs to stir and flip the chicken, or serve it cold.

Air Fryer Chicken Nuggets

Servings: 4
Cooking Time: 20 minutes

Ingredients:
- 1 lb boneless skinless chicken breasts cut into 2 inch pieces
- 2 eggs beaten

- ¼ cup whole wheat flour
- ¼ cup panko breadcrumbs
- ¼ cup breadcrumbs
- ¼ cup parmesan cheese
- 1 teaspoon salt
- ½ teaspoon onion powder
- ½ teaspoon garlic powder

Directions:

1. Cut chicken into 1.5 to 2 inch 'nugget-shaped' pieces.
2. Grab three bowls. In the first bowl, add the eggs.
3. Add the flour to the second bowl.
4. Add the panko, breadcrumbs, parmesan cheese, salt, onion powder and garlic powder to the third bowl and mix to combine.
5. Using tongs or a fork, toss chicken pieces to coat in the flour, then the egg, then the breadcrumb mixture. Place on a clean plate and repeat until all chicken bites are coated.
6. Heat your air fryer to 200°C/390°F. Working in batches, add the chicken nuggets to the air fryer basket and cook for 4 minutes.
7. Flip, and cook for 3 more minutes, or until cooked through and 165°F or no longer pink in the middle.
8. Repeat with all chicken nuggets until they are all cooked through.
9. Serve with ranch dressing, barbecue sauce, or your favorite dipping sauce.

NOTES

Storage

Store in an air tight container in the fridge for up to 4 days.

Freezing

uncooked chicken nuggets- after breading the chicken, arrange on a baking sheet. Freeze for 2-3 hours, until frozen solid. Transfer to a meal prep container or freezer bag and freeze for up to 3 months.

cooked chicken nuggets– place in a meal prep container or freezer bag. Freeze for up to 3 months.

Reheating

Reheat at 200°C/390°F for 2-3 minutes, until warmed through and crispy.

Air Fryer Chicken Thighs

Servings: 4
Cooking Time: 25 minutes

Ingredients:

- 4 chicken thighs (bone-in, skin-on or boneless, skinless)
- spray oil
- Rub
- 1 teaspoon onion powder

- 1 teaspoon garlic powder
- ½ teaspoon paprika
- ½ teaspoon pepper (optional; can be a touch spicy for kids)
- ½ teaspoon salt
- ½ teaspoon thyme leaves

Directions:

1. Boneless skinless thighs
2. Place chicken thighs on a plate. Spray on both sides with spray oil.
3. Stir together the rub, and sprinkle over the chicken. Press it on with your hands (to get it to stick properly), flip the thighs, and repeat on the other side.
4. Heat air fryer to 390°F/200°C.
5. Place two of the chicken thighs in the bask of the air fryer, making sure they are spread out and not curled up. Cook for 4 minutes.
6. Flip, and cook for 4 more minutes, or until a digital thermometer stuck into the thickest part reads 165°F.
7. Remove the chicken from the air fryer, cover, and rest for 5 minutes before serving.
8. Bone-in, skin-on thighs
9. Place chicken thighs on a plate. Spray on both sides with spray oil.
10. Stir together the rub, and sprinkle over the chicken. Press it on with your hands (to get it to stick properly), flip the thighs, and repeat on the other side.
11. Heat air fryer to 390°F/200°C.
12. (optional) Place 2 pieces of bread, torn, into the bottom of the air fryer, under the basket.
13. Place all four chicken thighs into the basket, spreading them out as much as possible. Cook for 15 minutes.
14. Flip the chicken carefully, and cook for another 8-10 minutes, until an internal temperature of at least 165°F is reached.
15. Remove from the air fryer, and let chicken rest (uncovered) for 5 minutes before serving.

NOTES

Storage

Store cooked chicken thighs in an air tight container in the fridge for up to 4 days.

Reheat

Reheat in the air fryer at 390°F/200°C for 3 minutes (boneless) or 5 minutes (bone-in), until crispy and heated through.

Crispy Air Fryer Chicken Tenders

Servings: 4
Cooking Time: 10 minutes

Ingredients:
- 1 lb chicken tenders
- 1 tablespoon olive oil

- Breading
- ¼ cup bread crumbs
- ½ teaspoon salt
- ½ teaspoon paprika
- ¼ teaspoon black pepper
- ⅛ teaspoon garlic powder
- ⅛ teaspoon onion powder
- 1/16 teaspoon cayenne pepper

Directions:

1. Heat air fryer to 390°F / 200°C.
2. Brush chicken tenders lightly with olive oil on both sides.
3. Stir together the breading. Using tongs, dredge the chicken in the breading, flipping over and repeating multiple times until the tenders are completely coated. Shake off excess breading and place in the air fryer right away.
4. Cook in batches of 3-4 at a time, making sure the chicken strips don't touch each other. Cook for 3 minutes, flip, and 2 minutes on other side before checking that they've reached an internal temperature of 165°F and removing from the air fryer.
5. To prepare ahead
6. These chicken tenders can be cooked 2-3 days ahead and stored in the fridge. To re-heat, place in the air fryer and heat for 2-3 minutes until they are crispy again.

NOTES

Storage

Chicken may be cooked up to 3 days ahead, and re-heated in the air fryer for 2-3 minutes until heated through and crispy.

Freezer

Chicken may be breaded ahead and frozen raw: first freeze on a baking sheet 2-3 hours, then transfer to a freezer bag. Freeze for up to 3 months

Air Fryer Chicken Breast

Servings: 4

Cooking Time: 6 minutes

Ingredients:

- 1 lb boneless skinless chicken breasts roughly 2 large
- 1 tablespoon olive oil
- Breading
- ¼ cup bread crumbs
- ½ teaspoon salt
- ¼ teaspoon black pepper

- ½ teaspoon paprika
- ⅛ teaspoon garlic powder
- ⅛ teaspoon onion powder
- 1/16 teaspoon cayenne pepper

Directions:

1. Prepare - Heat air fryer to 390°F / 200 °C. Slice chicken breasts in half horizontally to make two thin chicken breast halves from each. Brush each side lightly with olive oil.

2. Bread - Stir together the breading ingredients. Dredge the chicken breasts in the breading multiple times until they are thoroughly coated.

3. Shake off excess breading, and place in a single layer in the air fryer (2 chicken breast halves at a time).

4. Cook - Shake off excess breading, and place in a single layer in the air fryer (2 chicken breast halves at a time). Cook for 4 minutes.

5. Flip- Flip, then cook for two more minutes. Precise cook time will depend on the size and thickness of your chicken breasts, so either check with a digital thermometer that chicken has reached 165°F or cut one in half.

NOTES

We recommend using regular breadcrumbs as opposed to panko as the seasonings mix in much better. For a gluten-free option, some readers have reported back that gluten-free bread crumbs were a success!

Storage

Fridge - Cool completely, then store in an air-tight container in the fridge for up to 3 days.

Freeze- while we haven't tested this particular recipe, we've had success in freezing other breaded chicken recipes (raw or cooked). Flash freeze the breaded chicken on a baking sheet for 2-4 hours, then transfer to a freezer bag or container for longer term storage (3 months). Cook from frozen or thaw first (we do not have precise cook times to cook from frozen).

Reheat - Reheat in a pre-heated air fryer at 390°F/200°C for 2-3 minutes, until heated through and breading becomes crispy again!

Air Fryer Chicken Wings

Servings: 4
Cooking Time: 25 minutes

Ingredients:
- 1 ½ lbs chicken wings & drumettes
- 1 tablespoon olive oil or avocado oil
- ¼ teaspoon black pepper
- ½ teaspoon salt

Directions:

1. Preheat - Heat the air fryer to 200°C/ 390°F. Place near a window or under a hood fan as chicken wings may produce grease which can smoke.

2. Prepare wings - Blot chicken wings with paper towel to remove any moisture. Toss chicken wings in olive oil, salt & pepper.

3. Air Fry - Place all the wings in the air fryer basket and cook for 25-35 minutes, shaking and tossing them up every 10 minutes.

4. Chicken wings are ready when they are golden brown on all sides and crispy. Enjoy immediately! These wings do not keep well.

NOTES

Storage

Air fryer chicken wings are best enjoyed immediately for the ultimate crispy texture. However, if you have leftovers they can be stored and reheated; but you should expect them to be a bit drier and less crispy after reheating.

Lemon Pepper Air Fryer Chicken and Broccoli

Servings: 4

Cooking Time: 10 minutes

Ingredients:
- 1 lb boneless skinless chicken breasts roughly 2 breasts; cut into 1.5 inch pieces
- 1 crown broccoli roughly 4 cups; cut into 1.5 inch pieces
- 1 tablespoon olive oil
- 2 teaspoons lemon pepper seasoning
- 1 teaspoon dried basil
- ¼ teaspoon salt

Directions:
1. Prepare chicken and broccoli- Toss chicken and broccoli in olive oil, then add the lemon pepper, basil and salt, and toss until evenly coated.

2. Arrange- Spread the chicken and broccoli on two trays of an oven-style air fryer or in a single layer in a basket-style air fryer. Chicken can be touching but should not be stacked.

3. Cook- Heat air fryer to 400°F/ 200°C. Add the sheets (or basket) to the air fryer, and cook for 5 minutes.

4. Flip- After 5 minutes, remove trays from the air fryer and use tongs to carefully stir up and flip the chicken. If using an oven-style air fryer, rotate trays so the top tray goes to the bottom and bottom tray to the top.

5. Cook for another 5-7 minutes, until chicken is cooked through and no longer pink in the middle.

6. Enjoy- serve in a pita, or with a starchy side dish. Yogurt is delicious drizzled over the chicken and broccoli.

NOTES

Storage

After cooking, cool and portion out into an air tight storage container. Store in the fridge for up to 4 days.

Reheating

When you are ready to eat, you can reheat in the microwave until steaming hot, or you can heat at 400°F in the air fryer for 3-5 minutes.

Crispy Air Fryer Chicken Taquitos

Servings: 4
Cooking Time: 15 minutes

Ingredients:
- 1 lb boneless skinless chicken breasts roughly 2 large chicken breasts
- 1 tablespoon olive oil
- ½ teaspoon cumin
- ½ teaspoon chili powder
- ½ teaspoon onion powder
- ½ teaspoon garlic powder
- ¼ teaspoon salt
- 2 cups shredded mozzarella
- 10 medium tortillas

Directions:
1. Prepare chicken breast- In a medium-sized bowl, toss chicken in olive oil to coat. Sprinkle with cumin, chili powder, onion powder, garlic powder and salt on both sides.
2. Cook chicken breast- Heat air fryer to 400°F for 5 minutes before adding chicken. Cook for 10 minutes, flipping halfway through. Ensure chicken has reached 165°F when checked with an instant read thermometer in the thickest portion.
3. Remove chicken from air fryer, set aside and allow it to cool slightly.
4. Prepare filling- Shred the chicken with two forks, and allow to cool slightly. Stir in the cheese until well combined.
5. Roll- Place roughly ½ cup of the chicken/cheese mixture in the middle of a medium-sized flour tortilla. Roll it up tightly, and place seam side down on a plate. Repeat.
6. Cook- Heat air fryer to 400°F for at least 5 minutes. Carefully add the taquitos to the basket, placing them seam side down. Spray tops of tortillas with spray oil and cook for 3-4 minutes, until golden and crispy
7. Serve- Top with fresh tomatoes, lettuce, avocado, sour cream or salsa, and enjoy!

Duck Legs In Air Fryer

Servings: 2
Cooking Time: 18 minutes

Ingredients:
- 2 Duck Legs
- 120 g Packet Sweet Chilli Sauce
- 1 Tsp Ginger Puree

- 2 Tsp Garlic Puree
- ½ Tsp Chinese Five Spice
- Salt & Pepper

Directions:

1. Score your duck legs to create flavour pockets for your marinade.
2. Season the duck generously with salt and pepper.
3. Then transfer the duck legs into a mixing bowl with the other ingredients and mix well with your hands.
4. Line your air fryer with paper liner and add two duck legs over the paper, making sure the duck legs are not on top of each other.
5. Air fry the duck legs for 18 minutes at 180c/360f or until cooked to your liking.
6. For a sticky duck leg, we recommend when the air fryer has 5 minutes left, that you brush some extra marinade over the duck skin.

Air Fryer Chicken Fajitas

Servings: 2
Cooking Time: 18 minutes

Ingredients:

- 2 Medium Chicken Breasts
- 2 Mixed Peppers any colours
- 1 Medium Red Onion
- 1 Tbsp Extra Virgin Olive Oil
- 2 Tbsp Fajitas Seasoning
- Salt & Pepper

Directions:

1. Peel the onion and slice into thin strips. Also slice into strips the chicken breast and the two peppers.
2. Place the chicken and veggies into a bowl with the olive oil and seasonings and mix well with your hands.
3. Place the veggies into the air fryer basket and spread it out, leaving the chicken in your bowl for now. Air fry the veggies at 180c/360f for 6 minutes.
4. Shake the air fryer, add the chicken and continue to air fry at the same temperature for a further 12 minutes or until the chicken is cooked. Then serve with your favourite sides.

Marinated Chicken In Air Fryer

Servings: 4
Cooking Time: 20 minutes

Ingredients:

- For one batch of chicken marinade

- 4 Medium Chicken Breasts
- **1 – Coriander/Cilantro Lime**
- 2 Tbsp Lime Juice
- 3 Tbsp Extra Virgin Olive Oil
- 2 Tbsp Clear Honey
- 1 Tsp Garlic Purée
- 2 Tbsp Finely Chopped Fresh Coriander/Cilantro
- Salt & Pepper
- **2 – Curry Yoghurt**
- 1 Tsp Garlic Purée
- 1 Tsp Ginger Puree
- 1 Tbsp Extra Virgin Olive Oil
- 3 Tbsp Greek Yoghurt
- 2 Tsp Mild Curry Powder
- 1 Tsp Ground Turmeric
- 1 Tsp Ground Cumin
- 1 Tsp Dried Coriander/Cilantro Leaf
- Salt & Pepper
- **3 – Greek Kebabs**
- 2 Tsp Garlic Purée
- 1 Tbsp Balsamic Vinegar
- 1 Tbsp Lemon Juice
- 1 Tbsp Extra Virgin Olive Oil
- 2 Tbsp Greek Yoghurt
- 2 Tsp Dried Oregano
- Salt & Pepper
- **4 – Hawaiian Summer**
- 2 Tbsp Pineapple Juice
- 2 Tbsp Barbecue Sauce
- 1 Tbsp Tomato Ketchup
- Juice and Finely Grated Zest of 1 Lime
- 1 Tbsp Extra Virgin Olive Oil
- 1 Tsp Garlic Purée
- 1 Tsp Ginger Purée
- 1 Tsp Ground Cumin
- 1 Tsp Smoked Paprika
- Salt & Pepper
- **5 – Honey & Garlic**
- 1 Tbsp White Wine Vinegar
- 1 Tbsp Extra Virgin Olive Oil

- 2 Tsp Garlic Purée
- 100 g Clear Honey
- ¼ Tsp Dried Parsley
- Salt & Pepper
- 6 – Moroccan Spice
- 1 Tsp Garlic Purée
- 1 Tsp Ginger Purée
- 2 Tsp Tomato Purée/Paste
- 1 Tsp Harissa Paste
- 4 Tbsp Passata
- 2 Tbsp Extra Virgin Olive Oil
- 1 Tsp Dried Coriander/Cilantro Leaf
- 1 Tsp Ground Cumin
- 1 Tsp Smoked Paprika
- ¼ Tsp Ground Cinnamon
- Salt & Pepper
- 7 – Sweet Chilli
- 240 g Sweet Chilli Sauce
- 1 Tsp Garlic Purée
- 1 Tsp Ginger Purée
- 2 Tsp Soy Sauce
- ¼ Red Bell Pepper/Capsicum, Finely Chopped
- ½ Tsp Chinese 5-Spice Powder
- Salt & Pepper

Directions:

1. Use the ingredients from the chicken section and mix with 1 marinade. Or you can make 7* the marinades and then mix and match with 7* lots of protein.
2. Bagging. If using a bag holder and zip loc bags place the marinade into the bag, shake it all about and seal. If saving for the freezer, label it up and freeze it flat.
3. If preparing in the foil tray, add the marinade, mix in the chicken ingredients, fridge or freeze for later and then air fry when ready.
4. If using the zip loc method, transfer the contents of the bag to a paper liner and air fry. Or if using the tray containers, when ready transfer to the air fryer.
5. To air fry, set the temperature to 180c/360f and air fry for 15 minutes for small breasts, 20 minutes for medium and 25 minutes for large.
6. Always perform an internal temperature of the chicken at the thickest part and make sure its 70c/160f or above before serving.
7. Then slice your chicken and its ready for enjoying.

Whole Chicken In Air Fryer

Servings: 4

Cooking Time: 45 minutes

Ingredients:
- 1 Medium Whole Chicken
- 1 ½ Tbsp Dried Mixed Herbs
- Olive Oil Spray
- Salt & Pepper

Directions:
1. Let's cook a whole chicken in air fryer. Start by placing the whole chicken, breast side down, on a chopping board. Spray with olive oil into all the visible skin, then sprinkle half the mixed herbs over the chicken and season with salt and pepper. Transfer to the air fryer, breast side down.
2. Air fry at 180c/360f for 25 minutes and then flip the chicken over. The best way to do this is to place a fork in the cavity. Then spray the top with olive oil.
3. Sprinkle with the remaining dried seasoning, along with a generous sprinkle of salt and pepper.
4. Air fry at the same temperature for a further 20 minutes or until the chicken reads an internal temperature of 70c/160f or above.

VEGETABLES & SIDE DISHES RECIPES

Air Fryer Broccoli

Servings: 4
Cooking Time: 6 minutes

Ingredients:
- 1 head of broccoli
- 2 tablespoons butter melted
- 1 clove garlic minced
- salt and pepper to taste
- 1/4 cup Parmesan cheese freshly grated
- additional parmesan cheese for serving
- pinch of red pepper flakes optional

Directions:
1. Preheat your air fryer to 400 degrees.
2. Cut broccoli into florets and set aside.
3. Mix together melted butter, minced garlic, salt, pepper, and red pepper flakes (if using).
4. Add the broccoli and mix to combine thoroughly.
5. Add the Parmesan cheese and mix again making sure to coat it evenly.
6. Place broccoli into the air fryer and cook for 6-8 minutes, shaking the basket halfway through.*
7. Remove broccoli from the air fryer and serve immediately.
8. Add additional Parmesan cheese on top once served.

Easy Air Fryer Asparagus

Servings: 4
Cooking Time: 8 minutes

Ingredients:
- 1 bundle asparagus
- 1 teaspoon olive oil
- 1/8 teaspoon garlic salt
- 1 Tablespoon Parmesan cheese powdered or grated
- pepper to taste

Directions:
1. Preheat your air fryer to 400 degrees.
2. Clean asparagus and pat dry. Cut 1 inch off the bottom to take off the woody stems.

3. Lay asparagus in a single layer in air fryer and spritz with oil.
4. Sprinkle garlic salt evenly on top of asparagus. Season with pepper and then add a little Parmesan cheese across the top.
5. Cook at 400 degrees for 7-10 minutes. Thinner asparagus may cook faster.
6. Once asparagus is removed from the air fryer, add a little more Parmesan cheese to finish it off!
7. Enjoy immediately.

Air Fryer Frozen Onion Rings

Servings: 2
Cooking Time: 4 minutes

Ingredients:
- 6 ounces of frozen onion rings about 1/2 a bag of Alexia onion rings

Directions:
1. Preheat your air fryer to 350 degrees for about 3 minutes.
2. Place onion rings in the air fryer, stacking if needed.*
3. Cook air fryer onion rings for 4 minutes, shaking the basket halfway through.**
4. Remove from the air fryer and enjoy immediately.

Air Fryer Brussel Sprouts

Servings: 4
Cooking Time: 10 minutes

Ingredients:
- 1 pound brussel sprouts trimmed and halved
- 2 tablespoons oil
- 1/4 teaspoon salt
- pepper to taste
- 2 tablespoons sweet chili sauce like Frank's Red Hot Sweet Chili Sauce
- pinch of red pepper flakes

Directions:
1. Preheat air fryer to 400 degrees.
2. Add halved Brussel sprouts into a bowl with oil, salt, and pepper. Mix to combine.
3. Place Brussel sprouts into the air fryer and set the bowl aside. It's okay if they overlap, just do not fill your air fryer more than halfway.
4. Cook brussels sprouts for 8-10 minutes, shaking the basket halfway through.
5. Remove brussel sprouts from the air fryer and put them back into the bowl. Toss in sweet chili sauce and add red pepper flakes if using. Mix to combine.

6. Put brussel sprouts back into the air fryer and cook for 1-2 minutes to heat up the sauce.
7. Remove from the air fryer and enjoy immediately.

Air Fryer Cauliflower Steaks

Servings: 2
Cooking Time: 14 minutes

Ingredients:
- 1 small cauliflower
- 2 tablespoons oil
- ½ teaspoon garlic powder
- ½ teaspoon onion powder
- pinch salt and pepper

Directions:
1. Preheat your air fryer to 350F.
2. Cut the cauliflower in half through the stem, then cut two thick steaks, about 1½ inches in thickness. Keep the leftover cauliflower for another recipe.
3. Mix together the oil, garlic powder, onion powder and salt and pepper.
4. Brush the oil mix all over the cauliflower steaks and place in the air fryer basket.
5. Cook at 350F for 14 minutes, flipping halfway so they get crisp all over.

Easiest Air Fryer Kale Chips

Servings: 2
Cooking Time: 3 minutes

Ingredients:
- 2 cups kale Use Curly kale. Wash the kale well.
- ½ teaspoon olive oil Avocado oil. Olive oil can be used instead, if needed.
- ¼ teaspoon salt Preferably coarse sea salt, but any salt will do.

Directions:
1. Remove the thick inner rib from each kale leaf.
2. Tear kale into pieces.
3. Place kale pieces in a single layer in an air fryer basket fit for your air fryer.
4. Lightly coat each piece with oil.
5. Sprinkle with salt.
6. Air fry at 325° for 3-4 minutes. If your air fryer is pre-heated, they probably won't take longer than 3 minutes, so keep a close eye on them.
7. Let cool to room temperature. Enjoy!

Air Fryer Kielbasa and Potatoes

Servings: 4
Cooking Time: 24 minutes

Ingredients:
- 4 medium potatoes
- 1 large onion
- 1 red bell pepper
- spray oil
- 1/2 teaspoon garlic powder
- 1/2 teaspoon salt
- 1/4 teaspoon pepper
- 1 cup barbecue sauce use your favorite
- 1 pound kielbasa

Directions:
1. Wash and chop the potatoes, onions and red pepper. Cut them into bite sized pieces and put them into a bowl.
2. Spray the vegetables in the bowl with a few squirts of spray oil. Then add the garlic powder, salt and pepper to the bowl and toss to mix everything.
3. Add the barbecue sauce to the bowl and mix again. Then pour the contents of the bowl into the air fryer basket.
4. Set the air fryer for 400 F for 16 minutes. Shake the basket once or twice as it cooks to make sure it cooks evenly.
5. Whilte the vegetables cook use a sharp, serrated knife to cut the kielbasa into 1/2 inch pieces.
6. After the 16 minutes are up add the kielbasa to the air fryer basket and mix everything together.
7. Air fry at 400 F for another 8 minutes. The potatoes should be browned and tender and the kielbasa should be crispy around the edges.
8. Put the meal on a serving platter and drizzle it with more barbecue sauce.

Air Fryer Fingerling Potatoes Recipe

Servings: 4
Cooking Time: 15 minutes

Ingredients:
- 1 pounds fingerling potatoes about 10
- 1/2 tablespoon olive oil
- 1/2 teaspoon salt or to taste

- 1/2 teaspoon black pepper or to taste
- 2 tablespoons Parmesan cheese

Directions:
1. Scrub potatoes and pat them dry with a kitchen towel. Then cut them in half lengthwise.
2. Put them in a medium bowl and drizzle with the olive oil.
3. Sprinkle on the salt, ground pepper, and parmesan cheese.
4. Air fry at 400 F for 8 minutes. Then take the basket out and flip them over.
5. Air fry for another 5-8 minutes until they are browned and crispy on the outside.

Air Fryer Sweet Potato Wedges Recipe

Servings: 4
Cooking Time: 15 minutes

Ingredients:
- 1 large or 2 medium-sized sweet potatoes
- 1 tablespoon olive oil
- 1 tablespoon Everything but the Bagel Spices or your favorite spices

Directions:
1. Wash the sweet potatoes. Peeling is optional.
2. Cut them in half lengthwise. Put one of the halves flat on a cutting board and slice into wedges about ¼ inch thick. Repeat with the other half. Pat the sweet potato pieces dry with paper towels.
3. Put the wedges in a medium bowl. Add the oil and the spices and mix everything together.
4. Place the sweet potato wedges in the air fryer basket. You need to cook them in a single layer, so you might have to cook them in 2 to 3 batches.
5. Close the air fryer and cook at 370 °F for 10-15 minutes, turning halfway through cooking. The exact cooking time will depend on how thick they are. They are done when they start to look wrinkled with brown edges.
6. Serve with your favorite dipping sauce, like ranch dressing, ketchup, or BBQ sauce.

Air Fryer Shishito Peppers

Servings: 4
Cooking Time: 6 minutes

Ingredients:
- 15-20 shishito peppers about 4 ounces
- spray oil
- 1/4 teaspoon salt
- 1/4 teaspoon black pepper optional

- For Lemon Aioli Dip
- 1/2 cup mayonnaise
- 1 tablespoon fresh lemon juice
- 1 garlic clove minced

Directions:

1. Peppers
2. Rinse the peppers and pat them dry. Put them in a bowl and spray them with a little bit of oil.
3. Put them in an air fryer basket in a single layer. Air fry them at 390 degrees F for 6 minutes.
4. The peppers should be wrinkled with the skin starting to peel and some brown spots. If you want them darker return them to the air fryer for 1-2 additional minutes.
5. Sprinkle the charred peppers with salt and pepper if desired. Make a dipping sauce or serve them with lemon wedges and top them off with a squeeze of lemon juice.
6. Garlic Aioli Sauce
7. Whisk the mayonnaise, lemon juice and minced garlic together. Serve as a dipping sauce for the peppers.

Roasted Air Fryer Carrots Recipe

Servings: 6
Cooking Time: 20 minutes

Ingredients:
- 2 pound carrots
- 3 tablespoons butter or olive oil
- 2 tablespoons honey or maple syrup
- 1 tablespoon fresh thyme or 1 teaspoon dried
- ½ teaspoon salt
- 1 teaspoon black pepper

Directions:

1. Wash and peel the carrots. Then chop them into 1-inch pieces.
2. Put the butter in a large bowl. Microwave it until melted. Then whisk in the honey, half the thyme leaves, salt & pepper. Add prepared carrots, and toss to coat.
3. Add carrots and sauce to the basket in a single layer. Roast at 375 degrees F for 10 minutes. Then pull out the basket and shake it or stir to ensure even doneness. Cook for another 10 minutes or until tender and lightly caramelized.
4. Once done, use tongs to remove the carrots to a serving platter. Sprinkle with the remaining thyme leaves. Pour the accumulated juices into a bowl for serving.

Air Fryer Red Potatoes Recipe

Servings: 4

Cooking Time: 20 minutes

Ingredients:
- 1 pound red potatoes
- 1/2 tablespoon olive oil
- 2 teaspoons Everything Bagel Seasoning
- salt and black pepper to taste
- Other suggested seasoning variations
- Classic - 1 teaspoon garlic powder and 1 teaspoon salt
- Southwest - 1 teaspoon chili powder and 1 teaspoon cumin and salt to taste
- Italian - 2 teaspoons Italian seasoning and 1/2 teaspoon of salt
- Cajun - 2 teaspoons Cajun seasoning and salt to taste

Directions:
1. Cut the potatoes into quarters or dice them into smaller, 1-inch pieces.
2. Put them in a medium bowl. Drizzle with olive oil and then add the spices. Toss to mix everything together, so the spices coat all the pieces.
3. Put the potato mixture in the air fryer basket. Cook at 400 degrees F for 15 minutes for diced or 20 minutes for quartered. Take the basket out halfway through the cooking time and shake it to redistribute and ensure even cooking.
4. They are done when they are starting to brown outside and soft inside. To check for doneness, stick a fork in one, and if it goes in easily, they are ready to eat.

Air Fryer Butternut Squash

Servings: 6
Cooking Time: 15 minutes

Ingredients:
- 1 butternut squash or 4 cups diced
- 1 Tablespoon olive oil
- 1 teaspoon cinnamon optional
- 1/2 teaspoon salt

Directions:
1. Either buy cubed butternut squash or peel and cube it yourself. To cube it first cut off the ends, then stand it on end and use a vegetable peeler, not a knife, to remove the skin. A Y-peeler will work best for removing the thick skin.
2. Once it is peeled cut it in half and use a spoon to scoop out the seeds. Then dice it into 1 inch cubes.
3. Put the cubes in a bowl and add the olive oil, cinnamon and salt. Toss to mix.
4. Put the seasoned cubes in the air fryer basket. Don't fill it more than half full.
5. Set the air fryer at 400 F for 15 minutes. Take the basket out and shake it halfway through to redistribute

the pieces and ensure even cooking.

6. Check for doneness. It is done when a fork can easily pierce the cube. It will be brown on the edges and soft in the middle. If it needs more time return it to the air fryer another 3-5 minutes of cooking.

7. Serve right after cooking. If you'd like to make it sweeter drizzle it with 1 Tablespoon maple syrup or honey.

Air Fryer Yellow Squash

Servings: 4
Cooking Time: 10 minutes

Ingredients:
- 1 medium/small yellow squash
- 2 teaspoon olive oil
- 1/4 teaspoon salt
- 1/2 teaspoon pepper
- 1/2 teaspoon garlic powder

Directions:
1. Wash the yellow squash and slice it into rounds about 1/2 an inch thick. Then cut the rounds into halves or quarters.
2. Put the squash slices in a bowl. Drizzle the oil over top and add the salt, pepper and garlic powder.
3. Put the sliced in the air fryer basket, being careful not to overcrowd it. I can fit 1 1/2 - 2 medium sized squash in my 5.8 quart air fryer basket.
4. Air fry at 400 degrees F for 7 minutes. Check the squash and make sure it isn't browning too much. The squash is done when it is brown on the edges and not mushy in the middle.
5. I put my squash back in at 400 F for another 3 minutes and a total of 10 minute cooking time. But if you slice the squash more thinly it will cook more quickly. So check it after 7 minutes to be sure.

Air Fryer Broccoli

Servings: 4
Cooking Time: 6 minutes

Ingredients:
- 1 large bunch of broccoli 1 pound
- 1/2 Tablespoon sesame oil or olive oil
- 1/4 teaspoon salt
- 1/4 teaspoon garlic powder
- 2 Tablespoon water

Directions:
1. Wash the broccoli and cut it into bite sized pieces about 1 inch each. Include the stems if you like, they

taste delicious too.

2. Put the broccoli in a bowl and add the oil, salt and garlic powder. Toss everything to mix well and coat the broccoli.

3. Put 2 Tablespoons of water in the bottom of the air fryer, underneath the basket.

4. Add the broccoli to the basket and air fry it at 400 F for 6 minutes.

5. Check the broccoli and add a minute or two to the cooking time if you prefer it to be crispier.

Air Fryer Baked Potato

Servings: 3
Cooking Time: 30 minutes

Ingredients:
- 3 baking potatoes
- 1/2 Tablespoon olive oil
- 1/2 Tablespoon Kosher salt

Directions:
1. Wash and dry the potatoes.
2. Put the oil in a bowl and rub it on the potatoes.
3. Spinkle salt over the potatoes.
4. Put the potatoes in an air fryer basket, leaving space around them for air to circulate.
5. Cook at 400 F for 30 minutes, turning over after 15 minutes.
6. Test for the potatoes doneness by seeing if a fork goes into them easily. Or check the temperature with an instant read thermometer. They are done if they are at about 205 F.
7. Put them back in for another 10 minutes if necessary.

Air Fryer Acorn Squash Recipe

Servings: 4
Cooking Time: 25 minutes

Ingredients:
- 1 acorn squash
- 1 teaspoon olive oil
- 1/2 teaspoon salt
- 1/2 teaspoon cinnamon

Directions:
1. Wash the squash and dry it.
2. Use a large, sharp knife to cut it in half.
3. Scoop out all the seeds and insides using a spoon. You can leave it in halves or cut it into wedges if you

prefer.

4. Brush the cut sides with the olive oil and sprinkle on the salt and cinnamon.
5. Put the halves in the air fryer basket cut side up. Cook it at 370 degrees F for 20 minutes.
6. It is done when a fork goes easily into the flesh and the edges just start to brown.
7. Serve the halves as is or scoop the squash into a bowl and serve it mashed.

Air Fryer Mushrooms Recipe

Servings: 4
Cooking Time: 13 minutes

Ingredients:
- 1 pound mushrooms
- 1 tablespoon olive oil
- 1/3 teaspoon salt
- 1/3 teaspoon pepper
- 1/3 teaspoon garlic powder
- 1/3 teaspoon paprika
- 1/3 teaspoon dried herbs basil, thyme, oregano

Directions:
1. Preheat the air fryer to 390F. Wash and dry the mushrooms from excess moisture, and cut large mushrooms into 2-4 parts. Transfer to a medium bowl.
2. Add salt, spices, and olive oil to the mushrooms.
3. Mix everything thoroughly so that each piece of mushroom is evenly coated.
4. Put the mushrooms in the air fryer basket in one or two layers. Fry at 390F for 10 minutes.
5. After 10 minutes, shake the air fryer basket a few times while stirring the mushrooms. Cook for 3 more minutes.

Air Fryer Baby Potatoes

Servings: 6
Cooking Time: 14 minutes

Ingredients:
- 1 1/2 pounds whole baby potatoes
- 1 Tablespoon olive oil
- 1 - 4 teaspoons kosher salt depending on preference
- fresh herbs thyme, rosemary or sage, optional

Directions:
1. Wash and dry the potatoes. Make sure they are dry so that the skins get crispy.

2. Put the potatoes in a bowl and drizzle with the olive oil. Stir to coat the skins with oil. Add the salt and stir again.

3. Put the potatoes in the air fryer, making sure not to crowd the basket. Set it for 400 degrees F and cook for 14 minutes. Halfway through pull the basket out and shake to redistribute the potatoes.

4. Test the potatoes by inserting a fork into one of the larger ones. They are done when the fork goes in easily.

5. Cooking time will vary depending on what size your potatoes actually are. If they need more time cook them longer, testing every 3 minutes.

6. Toss with fresh herbs before serving if desired.

Air Fryer Corn on the Cob

Servings: 4
Cooking Time: 10 minutes

Ingredients:
- 4 ears of fresh corn
- 2 teaspoons olive oil
- 1/2 teaspoon salt
- 1/2 teaspoon pepper

Directions:
1. Peel the corn husks and remove the tassels and silk. Trim the ears if needed to fit in your air fryer basket. The corn should be in a single layer in the basket without overlapping or stacking.

2. Brush or spray the corn with olive oil. Don't use a commercial spray oil since it contains preservatives that can damage the coating on many air fryer baskets.

3. Sprinkle salt and pepper on the corn.

4. Air fry at 400 degrees F for 5 minutes. Then use tongs to flip the corn. Add more oil and seasoning if you like.

5. Air fry at 400 degrees F for another 5 minutes. Check to see if the corn is done by sticking a kernel with a sharp knife or fork. If it goes in easily the corn is done. If not cook it for another 2 minutes and check again.

Air Fryer Brussels Sprouts Recipe

Servings: 4
Cooking Time: 12 minutes

Ingredients:
- 1 pound Brussels sprouts
- 1 tablespoon olive oil
- ½ teaspoon salt

- ¼ teaspoon pepper
- ½ teaspoon garlic powder
- 1 tablespoon balsamic vinegar
- 1 tablespoon maple syrup

Directions:

1. Trim the stem end off the Brussels sprouts and cut them in half. Remove any brown outer leaves. If you have huge ones, cut them in quarters.
2. Put them in a mixing bowl and drizzle the sprouts with olive oil. Then sprinkle on the salt, pepper, and garlic powder and stir.
3. Place them in the air fryer, spreading them out in the basket. Air fry at 380 degrees F for 5 minutes.
4. Pull the basket out and shake it to redistribute the Brussels sprouts. Air fry for another 5-7 minutes until they are tender.
5. Scoop the veggies into a bowl and drizzle with balsamic vinegar and maple syrup.

Air Fryer Asparagus

Servings: 4
Cooking Time: 7 minutes

Ingredients:

- 1 bunch asparagus
- cooking spray
- 1 teaspoon Herbes de Provence seasoing
- 1 Tablespoon Parmesan cheese
- lemon wedges

Directions:

1. Wash the asparagus and then trim the edges off the bottom.
2. Spray the asparagus with a little bit of olive oil cooking spray.
3. cooking spray
4. Sprinkle the Herbes de Provence (or other desired seasoning on asparagus and toss to mix.
5. Put in an air fryer basket and cook at 360F for about 7 minutes.
6. Remove from the basket and sprinkle with Parmesan cheese.
7. Serve with lemon wedges.

Air Fryer Delicata Squash

Servings: 2
Cooking Time: 10 minutes

Ingredients:

- 1 delicata squash
- 1/2 Tablespoon olive oil
- 1/2 teaspoon rosemary
- 1/2 teaspoon salt

Directions:
1. Cut the delicata squash in half lengthwise. Scoop the seeds out and discard.
2. Slice the squash into slices about 1/4 inch thick.
3. Put the slices in a bowl and add the olive oil, rosemary and salt. Toss to mix well.
4. Put the squash slices in an air fryer basket. Set the air fryer at 400 F for 10 minutes. After about 5 minutes take the basket out and shake it to redistribute the squash and ensure even cooking.
5. Check the squash at the end of the 10 minutes. It should be cooked through and starting to brown around the edges. Put it back in for another 2-3 minutes at 400 F if it is not done.

Air Fryer Green Beans

Servings: 4
Cooking Time: 10 minutes

Ingredients:
- 1/2 pound fresh green beans
- olive oil or avocado oil in a spray bottle
- 1/2 teaspoon garlic powder
- 1/4 teaspoon salt

Directions:
1. Wash and dry the beans.
2. Cut the stem end off the beans. The curly tip can remain on.
3. Put the green beans in a bowl and spray with a little bit of cooking oil.
4. Add the garlic powder and salt. Toss the beans with tongs to coat.
5. Air fry the green beans at 360 degrees F for 8-10 minutes. Halfway through the cooking time remove the basket and shake to redistribute the beans.
6. If you want them crisper cook them for a minute or two longer.

Air Fryer Twice Baked Potatoes

Servings: 4
Cooking Time: 10 minutes

Ingredients:
- 2 cooked baked potatoes
- 2 Tablespoon sour cream

- 1/2 cup cheddar cheese
- 1 Tablespoon butter
- 2 slices bacon cooked

Directions:

1. Cut the baked potatoes in half and scoop out the insides into a bowl.
2. Add the sour cream, 1/4 cup of cheddar cheese and the butter to the bowl with the potatoes.
3. Mash the potatoes and other ingredients together with a potato masher until they have reached your desired consistency.
4. Spoon the filling back into the potato shells, mounding it to fit as necessary.
5. Refrigerate until ready to serve.
6. When you are ready to bake the potatoes put them in an air fryer basket. Cook at 400 F for 8 minutes.
7. Top the potatoes with the remaining 1/4 cup of cheddar cheese and bacon bits. Be careful not to touch the hot sides of the air fryer basket while you do this.
8. Return the potatoes to the air fryer and cook for 2 more minutes at 400 F to melt the cheese and crisp the bacon.

Air Fryer Eggplant

Servings: 4
Cooking Time: 10 minutes

Ingredients:
- 1 medium eggplant
- 1 Tablespoon olive oil
- 1/2 teaspoon salt
- 1/2 teaspoon garlic powder optional

Directions:

1. Cut the eggplant into cubes. There is no need to peel it.
2. Put the cubes in a bowl and toss with the oil, salt and garlic powder.
3. Put the eggplant in a single layer in the air fryer and cook at 400 F for 10 minutes. Shake the basket halfway through.

Air Fryer Sweet Potatoes

Servings: 2
Cooking Time: 35 minutes

Ingredients:
- 2 sweet potatoes
- 1/2 Tablespoon olive oil

- 1/2 Tablespoon kosher salt

Directions:

1. Wash the sweet potatoes well. Dry them thoroughly so they bake and not steam.
2. Use a fork to poke holes in the sweet potatoes.
3. Rub the olive oil all over the sweet potatoes and sprinkle them with the salt.
4. Put the prepared sweet potatoes in the air fryer basket, being sure not to crowd them.
5. Cook in the air fryer on 400 F for 30 minutes. Check the sweet potatoes for doneness and cook for another 5-15 minutes depending on their size. Sweet potatoes are done when they squish easily or when an instant read thermometer reads 200 F.
6. Serve with butter and cinnamon.

Air Fryer Garlic Knot Recipe

Servings: 5
Cooking Time: 5 minutes

Ingredients:
- 1 pound Pizza dough
- 1/4 cup unsalted butter
- 1 tablespoon garlic minced
- 1 teaspoon Italian seasoning
- 1/4 Cup grated Parmesan cheese

Directions:

1. Preheat your air fryer to 350 degrees F.
2. Melt the butter. Then combine it with the minced garlic in a small bowl.
3. Roll out the pizza dough on a floured cutting board. Use a pizza cutter to cut the dough into long strips with a pizza cutter. I shoot for 10-12 strips from 1 pound of dough.
4. Tie the strips into knots and place them in the air fryer basket. Keep them in a single layer so the air can circulate.
5. Use a pastry brush to coat them with the butter mixture. Sprinkle with Italian seasoning and parmesan cheese.
6. Air fry for 5-7 minutes.

Air Fryer Garlic Parmesan Corn Recipe

Servings: 4
Cooking Time: 10 minutes

Ingredients:
- 4 ears sweet corn

- 2 tablespoon unsalted butter softened
- 1/2 teaspoon salt
- 1/4 teaspoon black pepper
- 4 cloves garlic
- ¼ cup grated Parmesan cheese
- fresh parsley

Directions:
1. Husk the corn and cut it if needed to fit in the air fryer basket.
2. Spread the butter over the corn kernels.
3. Sprinkle the sweet corn with the salt, pepper, and minced garlic.
4. Put the corn in the air fry basket and cook at 400 degrees F for 10 minutes. Flip it once halfway through the cooking time.
5. Put the grated Parmesan on a plate and roll the corn ears in the cheese.
6. Serve with parsley or chives.

Air Fryer Sweet Potato Fries

Servings: 6
Cooking Time: 10 minutes

Ingredients:
- 2-3 Sweet Potatoes
- 2-3 Tablespoons olive oil
- 1/2 teaspoon salt
- 1/4 teaspoon black pepper
- 1/4 teaspoon paprika
- 1/2 teaspoon garlic powder

Directions:
1. Clean the sweet potatoes and pat them dry. Slice them into long and skinny french fry pieces about 1/4 inch to 1/2 inch wide. Thinner fries will be crispier.
2. Preheat the air fryer to 400 F.
3. Spray a little bit of olive oil on the air fryer basket to coat the bottom. This is separate from the 2-3 Tablespoons called for in the recipe.
4. Put the sweet potato pieces in a bowl. Drizzle them with the oil, then add the salt, pepper, paprika and garlic powder.
5. Toss everything so the fries are coated with the oil and seasonings.
6. Put the sweet potato fries in the air fryer basket, leaving room for the air to circulate. You might need to cook these in batches, depending on the size of your air fryer.
7. Cook at 400 F for 10 minutes. Halfway through take the basket out and shake it or flip the fries over.
8. After 10 minutes check the fries. They are done when they are wrinkled and just starting to get dark brown

on the edges.

9. If they need more time put them back in for another 1-5 minutes. The cooking time will depend on how thick the fries are and your air fryer's wattage.

10. Continue to cook another batch of fries. You can store the fries in a 220 F oven to keep them warm while you make more batches.

APPETIZERS & SNACKS RECIPES

Air Fryer Tofu

Servings: 4
Cooking Time: 10 minutes

Ingredients:
- 14 oz Extra Firm Tofu
- 3 tbsp Hoisin Sauce
- 2 tbsp Soy Sauce
- 2 tbsp Sugar or sugar substitute
- 1 tbsp Fresh Ginger
- 3 cloves Garlic minced
- 1/2 tsp Red Pepper Flakes
- 1 tbsp Vegetable Oil

Directions:
1. Marinate your extra firm tofu for up to 30 minutes in the ingredients listed above.
2. Add tofu to a well oiled 6" springform pan
3. Preheat the air fryer to 400F.
4. Cook for 10 minutes, shaking the air fryer basket half way through the cooking time.
5. Serve and enjoy!

Gluten Free Chip Recipe

Servings: 6
Cooking Time: 10 minutes

Ingredients:
- 2 cups shredded mozzarella cheese
- 1/2 cup Superfine Almond Flour
- 1/2 tsp Garlic Powder
- 1/4 tsp Ground Black Pepper

Directions:
1. In a microwave-safe bowl, warm the shredded cheese for 90 seconds or until it is melted.
2. Combine the melted cheese with the almond flour and spices.
3. Use your hands to form a ball of dough.
4. Spread the dough out extremely thin and use a pizza cutter to cut the dough into chip shapes.
5. Place the uncooked chips in the air fryer basket and cook for 8 minutes at 350F.

6. Remove them from the air fryer basket and allow them to cool completely before serving.

Meatball Casserole

Servings: 4
Cooking Time: 12 minutes

Ingredients:
- 12 meatballs
- 2 cups ricotta cheese
- 1 egg
- 1 cup shredded mozzarella cheese
- 1 cup Low Sugar Marinara Sauce
- 1/2 tsp Kosher Salt
- 1/4 tsp Ground Black Pepper
- 1 tsp Italian Seasoning
- 1/2 cup Cherry Tomatoes

Directions:
1. In a bowl, mix together the ricotta cheese, egg, salt, pepper, and Italian seasoning.
2. Drizzle half of the low carb marinara into the bottom of an oven-safe baking dish that will fit in your air fryer basket. Spread the ricotta mixture into the bottom of the dish on top of the sauce.
3. Place the thawed meatballs on top of the ricotta blend and add the remaining marinara sauce.
4. Cover the dish with aluminum foil and air fry the dish for 12 minutes, or until the meatballs are warmed through.
5. With 4 minutes remaining in the cooking time remove the aluminum foil, sprinkle on mozzarella cheese and cherry tomatoes and place the casserole back in the air fryer to finish.

Air Fryer Nachos (1)

Servings: 4
Cooking Time: 5 minutes

Ingredients:
- 2 cups nacho chips
- 1/2 cup chicken fajita meat
- 1/2 cup cherry tomatoes sliced
- 2 cups shredded cheese
- 1/4 cup black olives
- 1/4 cup sliced jalapeno

Directions:

1. Prepare the air fryer tray with nonstick spray such as olive oil. Layer the nacho chips in the bottom of the air fryer basket.
2. Top the chips with fajita meat, cheese, sliced tomatoes, and sliced jalapenos.
3. Cook the nachos on 320 degrees Fahrenheit for 3-5 minutes, checking during the last 2 minutes to ensure the cheese is melted and the tops of the chips are light golden brown.
4. Remove the nachos from the Air Fryer to a serving platter and add your favorite toppings such as a dollop of sour cream, sliced avocado, sliced black olives, and salsa.

NOTES

Store leftover nachos in an airtight container for up to 3 days in the refrigerator. For crispy nachos, sprinkle with extra cheese and reheat for 2-3 minutes.

Air Fryer Nachos (2)

Servings: 1
Cooking Time: 5 minutes

Ingredients:
- 1 ounce Quest Nacho Cheese Chips
- 1 Jalapeño Peppers
- 3 tbsp Onion
- 3 tbsp Tomatoes
- 1/2 cup Mexican Blend Shredded Cheese
- 1/2 Avocado
- 2 tbsp sour cream
- 1 tsp Cilantro
- 1 tsp lime juice

Directions:
1. Place a generous layer of Quest chips in the bottom of a silicone liner or other air fryer safe dish.
2. Top the chips with a generous amount of shredded cheese. Air fry at 350F for 5 minutes or until the cheese is melted and the chips are toasted.
3. While the air fryer nachos are cooking, dice up the onion, tomato, jalapeno, and avocado.
4. Plate the cheese-covered tortilla chips and garnish with the diced vegetables. Add a dollop of sour cream and a squeeze of lime juice. Sprinkle with cilantro and enjoy.

Maple Pecan Bars With Sea Salt

Servings: 8
Cooking Time: 25 minutes

Ingredients:

- For the Crust
- Non-Stick Cooking Spray
- 1/3 cup Butter softened
- 1/4 cup Brown Sugar firmly packed
- 1 cup All Purpose Flour
- 1/4 tea Kosher Salt
- For the Filling
- 4 TBS Butter (1/2 stick) diced
- 1/2 cup Brown Sugar
- 1/4 cup Pure Maple Syrup
- 1/4 cup Whole Milk
- 1/4 tea Vanilla extract
- 1 1/2 cup Pecans Finely Chopped
- 1/4 teaspoon Flaked Sea Salt for Topping

Directions:

1. For the Crust
2. Line a 8x8-inch square baking pan with foil, leaving a couple of inches of overhang. Spray the foil with nonstick baking spray.
3. In a medium bowl, combine the butter and brown sugar. Beat with an electric mixer on medium-low speed until light and fluffy. Add the flour and salt and beat until thoroughly combined. Transfer the mixture (it will be crumbly) to the prepared pan. Press it evenly into the bottom of the pan.
4. Transfer the mixture (it will be crumbly) to the prepared pan. Press it evenly into the bottom of the pan. (use the bottom of a coffee mug to help press it in the pan if needed.)
5. Place the pan in the air-fryer basket. Set the air fryer to 350°F for 13 minutes. When the crust has 5 minutes left to cook, start the filling.
6. For the Filling
7. In a medium saucepan, combine the butter, brown sugar, maple syrup, and milk. Bring to a simmer, stirring occasionally. When it begins simmering, cook for 1 minute. Remove from the heat and stir in vanilla and finely chopped pecans.
8. Carefully pour the filling evenly over the crust, gently spreading with a rubber spatula so the pecans and liquid are evenly distributed.
9. Set the air fryer for 12 minutes or until mixture is bubbling. (The center should still be slightly jiggly–it will thicken as it cools.)
10. Remove the pan from the air fryer and sprinkle with the salt. Cool completely on a wire rack. When cooled to room temperature, transfer the pan to the refrigerator. Use the foil overhang to remove from the pan and cut into 8 bars.
11. Serve at room temperature.

Air Fryer Corn Dogs

Servings: 4
Cooking Time: 8 minutes

Ingredients:
- 4 hot dogs
- 1/2 cup yellow cornmeal
- 1/4 cup all purpose flour
- 2 tsp granulated sugar
- 1 tsp kosher salt
- 1 tsp baking powder
- 1/2 cup buttermilk
- cooking spray

Directions:
1. Turn on your air fryer to 375F and allow it to preheat
2. Place the cornmeal, eggs, buttermilk, sugar, salt, and baking powder in a tall glass and mix until smooth.
3. Starting from one end, push the skewer into the middle of the hot dog lengthwise 3/4 of the way.
4. Roll the skewered hot dog in a shallow dish of flour until well coated.
5. While holding the skewer, carefully dip the flour coated hot dog into the tall glass of batter.
6. Add the battered corn dogs to the preheated air fryer basket, leaving plenty of room between them.
7. Cover the corn dogs with a light layer of cooking spray to help them crisp.
8. Air fry for 8 minutes, flipping half way through and coating the other side with cooking oil.

Air Fryer Green Beans with Bacon

Servings: 4
Cooking Time: 10 minutes

Ingredients:
- 3 cups Frozen Cut Green Beans
- 3 slices Bacon diced
- 1/4 cup Water
- 1 teaspoon Kosher Salt
- 1 teaspoon Ground Black Pepper

Directions:
1. Place the frozen green beans, onion, bacon, and water in a 6 x 3 inch heatproof pan.
2. Place the pan in the air fryer basket. Set air fryer to 375°F for 15 minutes.
3. Raise the air fryer temperature to 400°F for 5 minutes. Add salt and pepper to taste and toss well.
4. Remove from the air fryer and cover the pan. Let it rest for 5 minutes and serve.

Brussel Sprouts with Bacon

Servings: 4

Cooking Time: 30 minutes

Ingredients:
- 1 pound brussels sprouts
- 3 slices Bacon
- 1 Red Onion. chopped
- 2 tbsp Olive Oil
- Kosher Salt to taste
- Ground Black Pepper to taste

Directions:
1. Cut each sprout in half and take out hte touch outer leaves.
2. Dice bacon into small bits.
3. Cut onion into pieces that are roughly the same size as the sprouts.
4. Take a quart Ziploc bag (or a bowl) and mix all of the ingredients together.
5. Line a baking sheet with foil and spread the mixture in an even, single layer.
6. Bake at 350 for 30-50 minutes, turning half-way through.
7. You may want to finish up by broiling them to get them properly caramelized. I precooked them ,and when it was time to reheat, I broiled them to get them crispy.

Goat Cheese Appetizer

Servings: 8

Cooking Time: 20 minutes

Ingredients:
- 2 slices Prosciutto
- 1/2 cup Goat Cheese soft
- 4 Mission Figs dried and chopped
- 2 teaspoons tarragon fresh and snipped, or basil
- 1 Eggs
- 1 tablespoon Water
- All Purpose Flour for flouring your work surface
- 1 sheet Frozen Puff Pastry thawed

Directions:
1. Place the prosciutto slices on a dry paper towel. Lay another towel on top. Cook for 1 minute on high in the microwave. Remove top paper towel and allow the prosciutto to cool (meat will be slightly flexible but

will crisp upon cooling). When completely cool, crumble prosciutto and set aside.

2. In a medium bowl, combine goat cheese, figs, crisped prosciutto, and tarragon. Stir until well-blended.

3. In a small bowl, beat egg and water with a fork and set aside. Lightly flour a work surface. Roll out the thawed puff pastry sheet to a 12x12-inch square. Using a pizza cutter, cut into 16 (3x3-inch) squares and then brush the edges of the squares with the egg mixture.

4. Place about 2 teaspoons of the goat cheese mixture in the center of each square. Fold the pastry over the filling to form triangles. Press the edges to seal. Crimp the edges with a fork.

5. Arrange 8 of the pastry triangles in the air fryer, leaving as much space as possible in between them. Set air fryer to 400°F for 10 minutes or until pastry is golden brown. Repeat with remaining pastry triangles.

6. Serve warm.

Perfect Air Fryer Cheese Grits Recipe

Servings: 6
Cooking Time: 7 minutes

Ingredients:
- 3/4 cup hot water
- 2/3 cup instant grits 2 packages
- 1 Eggs beaten
- 1 tablespoon butter melted
- 2 teaspoons minced garlic
- 1/2-1 teaspoon red pepper flakes
- 1 cup shredded sharp cheddar cheese or jalapeno jack cheese (4 ounces)

Directions:
1. In a 6-inch heatproof pan, mix together thewater, grits, beaten egg, butter, garlic, and red pepper flakes and mix well. Fold in the shredded cheese. You will have a soupy mixture.

2. Place the pan in the air fryer basket.

3. Set the airfryer to 400°F for 10-12 minutes until the grits have cooked and a knife inserted near the center comes out clean. Let stand for 5 minutes before serving to allow the grits to thicken.

4. If you want to make these in the oven, cook at 400F for 15-18 minutes, until a knife inserted near the center emerges clean. Let stand for 5 minutes before serving to allow the grits to thicken.

Savory Potato Patties

Servings: 4
Cooking Time: 10 minutes

Ingredients:
- 2/3 cup dry instant potatoes

- 1/4 cup Frozen Peas and Carrots defrosted
- 2 tablespoons chopped cilantro
- 1 tablespoon Oil
- 1/2 teaspoon Turmeric
- 1/4-1/2 teaspoon Cayenne Pepper
- 1/2 teaspoon Kosher Salt
- 1/2 teaspoon cumin seeds
- 1/4 teaspoon Ground Cumin
- 2/3 cup hot water

Directions:
1. In a medium bowl, mix all ingredients. Cover and let the mixture rest for 10 minutes. Mix well.
2. Spray the air fryer basket with oil.
3. Using your hands, make 12 round, flat patties with even edges. Place patties directly into the air fryer basket. (You may have to cook in two batches in a small air fryer).
4. Set air fryer at 400F for 10 minutes. At 5 minutes, spray with some vegetable oil, and let the patties finish cooking.

Air Fry Frozen Mozzarella Sticks

Servings: 2
Cooking Time: 8 minutes

Ingredients:
- 1 bag 16 Frozen Mozzarella Sticks
- Olive Oil Spray

Directions:
1. Place the frozen mozzarella sticks into the air fryer basket and spread them out.
2. Spray with extra virgin olive oil as this will help for the crispy texture.
3. Air fry the cheese sticks at 180c/360f for 8 minutes or until they are nice and crispy.
4. Then serve with your favourite dipping sauce.

Air Fryer Snack Bags

Servings: 4
Cooking Time: 20 minutes

Ingredients:
- 650 g Chicken Breast
- Salt & Pepper

Directions:

1. Choose your marinade and mix up the marinade, ready for adding to the chicken breasts.
2. Then use a foil tray, zip loc bag or even a bowl to mix the chicken breasts in the marinade. Add to the freezer with a label if keeping for later, or fridge for dinner tonight.
3. Place the chicken breasts in the air fryer either on a paper liner, foil tray etc and air fry for 15 minutes for small, 20 minutes for medium, 25 minutes for large at 180c/360f.
4. Allow to fully cool before slicing either thin slices or thick depending on how you like them.
5. Finally transfer to a bag and store in the fridge for up to 3 days or the freezer for 3 months. You can then rinse and repeat with different chicken marinades, or different proteins and have a great air fryer meal prep recipe to turn to time and time again.

Big Mac Tacos In Air Fryer

Servings: 2
Cooking Time: 15 minutes

Ingredients:
- 2 Mini Tortilla Wraps
- 2 Slices American Processed Cheese
- FOR THE BURGERS
- 250 g Lean Minced/Ground Beef
- 1 Tsp Mustard Powder
- 2 Tsp Dried Basil
- 1 Tsp Lightest Cream Cheese
- 1 Tbsp Grated Cheddar Cheese
- 1 Tbsp Finely Sliced Onion optional
- Salt & Pepper
- FOR THE BURGER TOPPINGS
- 1 Small Lettuce such as baby gem
- 1 Large Tomato
- ¼ Medium White Onion
- 10 Gherkin/Pickle Slices
- FOR THE BURGER SAUCE
- 1 Tsp Tomato Ketchup
- 2 Tbsp Mayonnaise
- 2 Tbsp Fat-Free Greek Yoghurt
- 1 Tsp Gherkin/Pickle Juice
- ½ Tsp English Mustard
- ¼ Tsp Smoked Paprika

Directions:
1. Place the burger ingredients into a mixing bowl and mix well with your hands.

2. Form the burgers into two quarter pounder burger patties and then place into the air fryer basket. Air fry your big mac burgers at 180c/360f for 12 minutes.
3. In the meantime, prep your big mac sauce. Add the sauce ingredients into a bowl and with a spoon mix together until you have a creamy burger sauce. Put to one side.
4. Also prep the salad garnish for on top of your burgers. We used sliced tomatoes, sliced onion, some lettuce and gherkins.
5. When the air fryer beeps remove the burgers and add a tortilla wrap to each air fryer drawer, or you can do one at a time. Spread a teaspoon of sauce on them and then press down the almost cooked burger. Add a teaspoon of sauce on top, then push down a slice of the processed cheese. Air fry for another 3 minutes at the same temperature or until the cheese is perfectly melted.
6. Remove the mac tacos by the wrap, this makes it easier.
7. Then load up your burgers with salad garnish and the remaining sauce before serving.

Hot Dogs In Air Fryer

Servings: 3
Cooking Time: 10 minutes

Ingredients:
- 3 Large Hot Dogs
- 3 Large Hot Dog Buns
- 1 Small White Onion
- Extra Virgin Olive Oil Spray
- Optional Sauces
- Tomato Ketchup
- Deli Mustard

Directions:
1. Peel and thinly slice your onion.
2. Add the onion into the air fryer basket and spray with olive oil. Air fry for 3 minutes at 200c/400f.
3. Shake the air fryer basket and move the onion to one side, then add the hot dogs to the other.
4. Air fry for another 5 minutes at 180c/360f.
5. Transfer the hot dogs to buns, add the onions on top and transfer back to the air fryer. Air fry the hot dogs for another 2 minutes at 200c/400f.
6. Transfer the hot dogs to plates and add ketchup and mustard before serving.

Air Fryer Potato Chips

Servings: 4
Cooking Time: 20 minutes

Ingredients:
- 4 Russet Potatoes
- 2 tbsp Olive Oil
- 1 tsp Kosher Salt
- 1/2 tsp Black Pepper
- 1 tsp Garlic Powder
- 1 tsp Paprika

Directions:
1. Prepare the Potatoes. Wash and slice the potatoes very thinly using a mandoline slicer for uniform thickness. Soak the slices in cold water for at least 30 minutes to remove excess starch, which helps in achieving crispiness.
2. Season the Chips. Drain the potato slices and pat them dry with a clean kitchen towel. In a bowl, toss the potato slices with olive oil, salt, garlic powder, paprika, and black pepper until evenly coated.
3. Air Fry the Chips. Preheat your air fryer to 360°F. Arrange the potato slices in a single layer in the air fryer basket, making sure they don't overlap (you may need to work in batches). Cook for about 15-20 minutes, flipping the chips halfway through, until they are golden brown and crispy.
4. Cool and Crisp Up. Let the chips cool on a wire rack for a few minutes after cooking. They will continue to crisp up as they cool.

BEEF, PORK & LAMB RECIPES

Honey Mustard Pork Chops

Servings: 4
Cooking Time: 8 minutes

Ingredients:
- 4 pork chops 1/2 inch thick
- 4 tablespoons Prepared Mustard
- 2 tablespoons Honey
- 2 tablespoons Minced Garlic
- 1 teaspoon Kosher Salt
- 1 teaspoon Ground Black Pepper
- Cooking Oil Spray

Directions:
1. In a large bowl, mix together the mustard, honey, garlic, salt, and pepper.
2. Add the pork chops and toss to coat with the sauce.
3. Spray the air fryer basket. Place the chops into the greased basket.
4. Set the air fryer to 350°F for 12 minutes or until pork is cooked through, flipping halfway through and spraying with oil again.

Spicy Lamb Sirloin Steak

Servings: 4
Cooking Time: 15 minutes

Ingredients:
- 1/2 Onion
- 4 slices Ginger
- 5 cloves Garlic
- 1 teaspoon Garam Masala
- 1 teaspoon ground fennel
- 1 teaspoon Ground Cinnamon
- 1/2 teaspoon Ground Cardamom
- 1/2 - 1 teaspoon Cayenne Pepper
- 1 teaspoon Kosher Salt
- 1 pound boneless lamb sirloin steaks

Directions:

1. Into a blender bowl, add all ingredients except the lamb chops.
2. Pulse and blend until the onion is minced fine and all ingredients are blended, about 3-4 minutes.
3. Place the lamb chops into a large bowl. Use a knife to slash into the meat and fat to allow the marinade to penetrate better.
4. Add the blended spice paste and mix well.
5. Allow the mixture to rest for 30 minutes or up to 24 hours in a refrigerator.
6. Let your air fryer to 330F for 15 minutes and place the lamb steaks in a single layer in the air fryer basket and cook, flipping half way through.
7. Using a meat thermometer, ensure that the meat has reached an internal temperature of 150F for medium well, and serve.

Sichuan Cumin Lamb

Servings: 4
Cooking Time: 10 minutes

Ingredients:
- For the Lamb:
- 1.5 tablespoons Ground Cumin
- 1 teaspoon Sichuan peppers (or 1/2 tsp cayenne)
- 1 pound lamb (preferably shoulder) cut into 1/2" by 2" pieces
- 2 tablespoons Vegetable Oil
- 1 tablespoon Soy Sauce
- 1 tablespoons Minced Garlic
- 2 Red Chili Peppers chopped
- 1 teaspoon Kosher Salt
- 1/4 teaspoon Sugar Or Other Sweetener Equivalent
- For finishing:
- 2 Chopped Green Scallions chopped
- 1 large handful chopped cilantro

Directions:
1. In a dry skillet, roast together 2 tablespoons of cumin seeds and 1 teaspoon of Sichuan red peppers if using until fragrant. When they have cooled, use a mortar and pestle and give them a rough grind.
2. Use a fork to poke holes into the lamb to allow the marinade to penetrate better.
3. In a large bowl or a Ziploc bag, marinate the lamb with the cumin and Sichuan pepper blend, oil, soy sauce, garlic, red chili peppers, salt, sugar and cayenne pepper (if using).
4. Set your air fryer to 360F for 10 minutes and place the marinated lamb in a single layer in the air fryer basket.
5. Using a meat thermometer, ensure that the lamb has reached an internal temperature of 145F and remove to a serving tray.

6. Mix in the chopped scallions and cilantro, and serve.

Air Fryer Ribs (1)

Servings: 4
Cooking Time: 1 hours

Ingredients:
- 1 rack baby back ribs (3-4 pounds)
- 1-2 Tablespoons yellow mustard
- 3 Tablespoons bbq seasoning
- 2 Tablespoons water (for the air fryer)
- ½ cup BBQ sauce
- 2 Tablespoons water (to mix with BBQ sauce)

Directions:
1. Preheat a 7-quart basket air fryer to 350°F for 5 minutes.
2. Pat 1 rack baby back ribs dry with a paper towel. Remove the membrane (also called silver skin) on the underside of the ribs. It is easiest to do this by slicing off a little corner of the membrane and then using a paper towel to grip it and pull it off.
3. Cut the ribs into four even pieces, do the best you can.
4. Brush the ribs all over with the 1-2 Tablespoons yellow mustard. I like to add a thin coating of about 1 Tablespoon, but use more if you like.
5. Rub 3 Tablespoons bbq seasoning all over.
6. Add 2 Tablespoons water to the bottom of the air fryer basket.
7. Arrange the ribs, overlapping into the air fryer, and make sure you can shut the basket properly; you may need to play around with them a little to make them fit.
8. Cook for 45 minutes to 60 minutes, flipping them around every 15 minutes. Add more water to the bottom if you think it's starting to smoke.
9. The ribs are done when an internal temperature reaches 180-190°F. Take them out of the air fryer and place them on a sheet tray.
10. Mix 1/2 cup BBQ sauce with 2 Tablespoons water. Brush this all over the ribs.
11. Place the ribs, bone side down, back into the air fryer, not touching. You will have to do this step in batches.
12. Cook for an additional 3-5 minutes until the bbq sauce is bubbly and caramelized. Serve immediately.

Air Fryer Ribs (2)

Servings: 4
Cooking Time: 10 minutes

Ingredients:

- 1 tablespoon Sesame Oil
- 1 teaspoon Minced Garlic
- 1 teaspoon Minced Ginger
- 1 tablespoon fermented black bean paste
- 1 tablespoon Shaoxing Wine
- 1 tablespoon dark soy sauce
- 1 tablespoon agave nectar or honey
- 1.5 pounds Spare Ribs cut into small pieces

Directions:

1. In a large mixing bowl, stir together all ingredients for the marinade.
2. Add the spare ribs and mix well. Allow the ribs to marinade for at least 30 minutes or up to 24 hours.
3. When you're ready to cook the ribs, remove the ribs from the marinade and place into the air fryer basket.
4. Set the air fryer at 375F for 8 minutes.
5. Check to ensure the ribs have an internal temperature of 165F before serving.

Air Fryer Meatballs

Servings: 5
Cooking Time: 5 minutes

Ingredients:
- 1 lb ground beef
- 1 egg
- ½ cup breadcrumbs
- 1 teaspoon worcestershire sauce
- ½ teaspoon salt

Directions:

1. Mix ingredients- in a bowl, combine the ground beef, salt, worcestershire, breadcrumbs and egg. Use your hands or a spatula to mix until just combined. Do not over-mix.
2. Roll meatballs- use a 1 tablespoon measuring spoon or cookie scoop to measure out portions, then roll in your hands to form a ball.
3. Cook- Preheat the air fryer for 5 minutes, then add the meatballs to the basket or tray.
4. Flip- Cook for 3 minutes, then flip (or give the basket a little shake). Cook for another 2 minutes, or until the meatballs reach 150°F

Air Fryer Burgers

Servings: 4
Cooking Time: 9 minutes

Ingredients:
- 1 lb lean ground beef
- 2 cloves garlic minced
- 1 teaspoon Worcestershire sauce
- ½ teaspoon salt
- 1 large egg
- ¼ cup breadcrumbs
- To serve
- 4 burger buns
- tomatoes
- lettuce
- mayonnaise

Directions:
1. Mix- In a bowl, combine the ground beef, garlic, worcestershire, salt and egg. When completely combined, add the breadcrumbs and mix until integrated evenly.
2. Form patties- Divide the mixture into four, then take ¼ of the mixture into the palm of your hand. Work it into a 3-4 inch diameter circular patty that is of even thickness across. Do not exceed 1 inch in thickness. Repeat until you have four patties.
3. Cook- Pre-heat the air fryer to 400°F for at least 5 minutes, then add the burger patties to the basket. Cook for 6 minutes, then flip and cook for another 3 minutes. Check the internal temperature has reached 160°F before removing from the air fryer.
4. Serve- Serve burger patties on a bun with mayonnaise, tomato slices, lettuce or your favorite burger toppings!

NOTES

Storage

After cooking, patties may be stored in an air tight container in the fridge for up to 4 days.

Reheating

Cook in a covered frying pan for 3-4 minutes per side, until heated through.

Freezing

Raw patties may be frozen on a baking sheet for 2-3 hours, then transferred to a freezer bag or meal prep container. Separate patties using strips of wax or parchment paper.

Herb Crusted Air Fryer Pork Tenderloin

Servings: 4
Cooking Time: 15 minutes

Ingredients:
- 1 tablespoon olive oil
- ½ teaspoon onion powder

- ½ teaspoon garlic powder
- ¼ teaspoon salt
- ¼ teaspoon pepper
- 1 teaspoon basil
- 1 teaspoon oregano
- 1 lb pork tenderloin

Directions:

1. Mix up spice blend- In a small bowl, mix together the onion powder, garlic powder, salt, pepper, basil and oregano.
2. Prep pork tenderloin- Use a knife to wiggle under the silver skin of the pork (the vein of fat and connective tissue along the top of the tenderloin). Carefully cut it off.
3. Next, brush all sides of the tenderloin with olive oil, then rub the spice blend in. It's important to use your hands to press the rub onto the surface of the pork to help it stick.
4. Cook- Pre-heat air fryer to 400°F for at least 5 minutes, then add the tenderloin to the basket or lower tray. Cook for 15 minutes, flipping halfway through.
5. Check temperature- Use an instant read thermometer to determine if the pork tenderloin is ready to come out of the air fryer:
6. medium rare- 145-150°F
7. medium- 150-155°F
8. medium well- 155-160°F
9. Rest- Transfer tenderloin to a cutting board before slicing. You can cover it with a dish if you'd like to keep it warmer. After resting, slice and enjoy!

NOTES

Storage

Pork tenderloin is best served fresh as it tends to dry out as it is stored.

To store, cool completely before storing in an air tight container in the fridge for up to 4 days.

Reheat

Heat in the microwave or in a covered frying pan over medium heat, or until steaming hot.

Chipolata Sausages In Air Fryer

Servings: 2
Cooking Time: 20 minutes

Ingredients:
- 12 pork chipolata sausages
- Air fryer part baked bread rolls optional
- Favourite Sauces optional

Directions:

1. Place the chipolatas in an air fryer and spread them out for an even cook.

2. Air fry the sausages for 8 minutes at 180c/360f or until brown to your liking.
3. If serving with part baked bread rolls you can also cook these for 6 minutes at 180c/360f.
4. Load up the bread rolls with the sausages and serve with your favourite sauces.

Meatballs In Air Fryer

Servings: 4
Cooking Time: 10 minutes

Ingredients:
- ½ Small Onion
- 450 g Minced/Ground Beef
- 450 g Minced/Ground Pork
- 2 Tsp Garlic Puree
- 1 Tsp Worcestershire sauce
- 1 Tbsp Tomato Ketchup
- 2 Tsp Tomato Puree/Paste
- 2 Tbsp Light Cream Cheese
- 1 Tsp Mustard Powder
- 2 Tsp Dried Oregano
- 2 Tbsp Mixed Herbs/Italian Seasoning
- Salt & Pepper

Directions:
1. Peel and finely dice your onion.
2. Load into a bowl everything including the onion you have just chopped.
3. Mix the mixture with your hands and then once thoroughly mixed form into meatball shapes.
4. Place the meatballs into the air fryer basket or drawer, spreading them out so they are on a single layer.
5. Air fry the meatballs at 180c/360f for 10 minutes or until cooked to your liking and then serve.

Air Fryer Steak Fajitas

Servings: 2
Cooking Time: 18 minutes

Ingredients:
- 1 Medium Sirloin Steak
- 2 Mixed Peppers any colours
- 1 Medium Red Onion
- 1 Tbsp Extra Virgin Olive Oil
- 2 Tbsp Fajitas Seasoning

- Salt & Pepper

Directions:

1. Peel the onion and slice into thin strips. Also slice into strips the steak and the two peppers.
2. Place the veggies into a bowl with the olive oil and seasonings and the steak and mix well with your hands.
3. Place the veggies into the air fryer basket and spread it out, leaving the steak in your bowl for now. Air fry the veggies at 180c/360f for 10 minutes.
4. Shake the air fryer, add the steak and continue to air fry at the same temperature for a further 8 minutes or until the steak is cooked to your liking. Then serve with your favourite sides.

Hamburgers In Air Fryer

Servings: 4
Cooking Time: 12 minutes

Ingredients:
- ¼ Medium White Onion
- 450 g Minced/Ground Beef
- 2 Tsp Dried Mixed Herbs/Italian Seasoning
- 2 Tbsp Light Cream Cheese
- 1 Tsp Garlic Purée
- 4 Cheese Slices
- Salt & Pepper
- 3 Ingredient Burger Sauce
- 2 Tbsp Pink Sauce
- ¼ Tsp Dijon Mustard
- 1 Tsp Gherkin Juice/Pickle Juice

Directions:

1. Thinly dice your onion.
2. Add to a bowl all the burger ingredients apart from the cheese and burger sauce.
3. Then mix well with your hands until everything is well mixed.
4. Portion into 4 burger patties and then spread out in your air fryer basket.
5. Air fry your burgers for 12 minutes at 180c/360f or until cooked to your liking.
6. If you want a cheese melting moment (who doesn't) then add cheese over the tops of the burgers 3 minutes before the end of the cooking time.
7. Then serve the burgers in burger buns with the burger sauce, salad and its also nice to serve with some coleslaw too.

Gammon Steak In Air Fryer

Servings: 2

Cooking Time: 23 minutes

Ingredients:
- For the steaks
- 450 g Gammon Steaks
- Sprinkle Black Pepper
- For the chips
- 4 Medium Potatoes
- 1 Tbsp Extra Virgin Olive Oil
- 2 Tsp Dried Parsley
- Salt & Pepper

Directions:
1. Start by peeling and chopping the potatoes into chunky chips. Add them to a bowl with your olive oil, parsley and a generous seasoning of salt and pepper. Place the chips into one of the dual drawers.
2. Carefully remove the gammon from the packaging and place them into the 2nd dual drawer, being careful that they don't break and overlapping slightly if needed.
3. Sync the drawers. Air fry the chips for 23 minutes and the gammon for 8 minutes, both at 180c/360f. Though give the chips a shake just as the gammon is about to start.
4. Serve your gammon steak and chips with an air fryer fried egg.

Thin Steak In Air Fryer

Servings: 2
Cooking Time: 8 minutes

Ingredients:
- 230 g Steaks half thickness of a regular steak
- Salt & Pepper

Directions:
1. Place your steak onto a plate or chopping board and season generously with salt and pepper.
2. Place the thin steaks into the air fryer basket, spreading them out side by side. Air fry at 180c/360f for 4 minutes.
3. When the air fryer beeps, turn the steak over with tongs and then season again and cook at the same time and temperature again.
4. Then use a spatula to remove them from the air fryer before serving.

BREAKFAST RECIPES

Bacon Egg And Cheese Biscuit Sandwich

Servings: 4
Cooking Time: 28 minutes

Ingredients:
- For The Biscuits
- 1 cup All Purpose Flour
- 1 1/2 tsp Baking Powder
- 1/4 tsp Kosher Salt
- 2 tbsp Unsalted Butter
- 1/2 cup Whole Milk
- For The Eggs
- 4 Eggs
- 1 tbsp Heavy Cream
- 2 tbsp Unsalted Butter
- For The Remaining Filling
- 12 slices Bacon
- 4 slices Cheddar Cheese
- 1/2 tsp Kosher Salt
- 1/4 tsp Black Pepper

Directions:
1. Prepare the Biscuit Dough. In a large mixing bowl, combine the flour, baking powder, and salt. Cut in the cold butter until the mixture resembles coarse crumbs. Stir in the milk until a soft dough forms.
2. Shape the Biscuits. Turn the dough out onto a lightly floured surface and gently knead it a few times. Roll the dough out to about 1/2-inch thickness and cut out circles using a biscuit cutter. Bake at 425F for 12-15 minutes.
3. Cook the Bacon. Make oven baked bacon or air fryer bacon for easy clean up.
4. Scramble the Eggs. Place butter into a skillet over low heat. Scramble eggs in a small bowl with a splash of heavy cream. Slowly pour the eggs into the skillet and stir continually until the eggs are fully cooked.
5. Assemble the Biscuits. Place a cooked bacon slice, scrambled egg, and shredded cheese on half of the biscuit rounds. Top with the remaining rounds and seal the edges.
6. Bake the Biscuits. Transfer the assembled biscuits to a baking sheet and bake in a preheated oven until golden brown and cooked through.
7. Serve and Enjoy. Let the biscuits cool slightly before serving. Enjoy them warm for the ultimate breakfast experience!

Air Fryer Pizza Roll Up Recipe

Servings: 8

Cooking Time: 8 minutes

Ingredients:
- 14 oz Refrigerated Pizza Dough
- 1 cup Pizza Sauce
- 2 cups Mozzarella Cheese
- 6 oz Pepperoni
- 2 tbsp Olive Oil
- 1 tbsp Italian Seasoning

Directions:
1. Roll Out the Dough. Start by rolling out the pizza dough into a rectangle on a lightly floured surface. Aim for about 1/4-inch thickness.
2. Spread the Sauce. Evenly spread pizza sauce over the dough, leaving a small border along the edges.
3. Add Cheese and Toppings. Sprinkle a generous layer of shredded mozzarella cheese over the sauce. Then, add your favorite pizza toppings. This is where you can get creative!
4. Roll It Up. Carefully roll up the dough, starting from the long edge. Roll it tightly to ensure your pinwheels hold together.
5. Slice into Pinwheels. Use a sharp knife to slice the rolled dough into pinwheels, about 1-inch thick.
6. Brush with Olive Oil. Lightly brush the tops of the pinwheels with olive oil, and sprinkle with Italian seasoning.
7. Air Fry to Perfection. Preheat your air fryer to 350°F. Place the pizza pinwheels in a single layer in the air fryer basket, making sure they don't touch. You may need to cook them in batches, depending on the size of your air fryer.
8. Cook Until Golden. Air fry the pinwheels for about 6-8 minutes, or until they are golden brown and crispy on the outside, and the cheese is melted on the inside.
9. Serve and Enjoy. Remove the pizza pinwheels from the air fryer, let them cool slightly, and then serve them with your favorite dipping sauce.

Air Fryer French Bread Pizza Recipe

Servings: 8

Cooking Time: 6 minutes

Ingredients:
- 1 loaf french bread
- 1 1/2 cups Pizza Sauce
- 2 cups shredded mozzarella cheese

- 1 cup miniature pepperoni
- 1/4 cup Sun Dried Tomatoes
- 1 tbsp Garlic Powder
- 1 tsp Italian Seasoning
- 2 tbsp Olive Oil

Directions:

1. Preheat the air fryer- Set your air fryer to preheat at 375F for a few minutes while you prepare the French bread pizza.

2. Slice the French bread- Cut the French bread loaf in half lengthwise. Then, slice each half into individual serving-sized pieces. This will make it easier to handle and ensure even cooking.

3. Prepare the toppings- While the air fryer preheats, gather your pizza toppings of choice and prepare them accordingly. Slice any vegetables, such as bell peppers or onions, and set aside.

4. Assemble the French bread pizza- Spread a generous amount of pizza sauce on each slice of the French bread, leaving a small border around the edges. Sprinkle a handful of shredded mozzarella cheese over the sauce. Add your desired toppings and sprinkle some additional cheese on top. For an extra flavor boost, sprinkle a pinch of dried Italian seasoning and garlic powder over the toppings.

5. Transfer to the air fryer- Carefully place the assembled French bread pizzas in a single layer inside the air fryer basket. Depending on the size of your air fryer, you may need to cook them in batches.

6. Air fry the French bread pizzas- Slide the air fryer basket back into the machine and cook the French bread pizzas at 375F for approximately 6-8 minutes or until the cheese is melted, bubbly, and lightly golden. Cooking times may vary depending on the air fryer model, so keep an eye on the pizzas to avoid burning.

7. Add some oil- Brush with olive oil (for added crispiness): If you prefer a slightly crispier crust, you can brush the outer edges of the French bread slices with a little olive oil before air frying.

8. Serve and enjoy- Once the French bread pizzas are done, carefully remove them from the air fryer. Allow them to cool for a few minutes before serving. Garnish with fresh basil leaves or a sprinkle of grated Parmesan cheese if desired. Enjoy your homemade French bread pizza straight from the air fryer!

Air Fryer Egg Rolls (1)

Servings: 12
Cooking Time: 20 minutes

Ingredients:
- 1 tablespoon olive oil
- 1 pound ground pork (453g)
- 3 cups cole slaw mix (about 200g)
- 2 green onions chopped
- 2 garlic cloves minced
- 1 teaspoon grated ginger

- 2 tablespoons soy sauce
- 2 teaspoons toasted sesame oil
- 12 egg roll wrappers

Directions:

1. Heat the olive oil in a large nonstick skillet over medium-high heat. Add the pork and cook, stirring often, until only a few pink pieces remain about 4 minutes.
2. Add the cole slaw mix, green onions, garlic, and ginger. Cook, stirring often, until the cabbage is tender, about 2 minutes. Stir in the soy sauce and sesame oil.
3. Working one wrapper at a time, position it so it makes a diamond shape on your work surface. Lightly dab the top corner with water.
4. Spoon 3 to 4 tablespoons of pork mixture in the center of the wrapper. Fold the bottom corner up over the filling. Fold the two side corners towards each other over the filling, then roll up to the top corner and gently press to seal. Place the egg rolls in the air fryer basket, and spray lightly with cooking spray or brush with more olive oil.
5. Air fry, in batches, at 350°F, flipping after 7 minutes, until golden brown and crispy, about 12 minutes total. Serve hot with your favorite dipping sauce.

Air Fryer Egg Rolls (2)

Servings: 4
Cooking Time: 8 minutes

Ingredients:
- 4 strips bacon
- 1 cup cooked hashbrowns
- 2 large eggs
- 4 egg roll wrappers
- 4 tbsp vegetable oil
- 1/2 cup cheddar cheese
- 1 tsp salt
- 1/2 tsp pepper

Directions:

1. Take one egg roll wrapper and lay flat with one corner pointed toward your belly button.
2. Place desired ingredients into the center of the egg roll wrapper in a straight line. It should be approximately 1 inch wide with a span the length of the egg roll wrapper diagonally, leaving 1/2 an inch without filling on each end.
3. Fold in the two corners of the egg roll far enough that the fold touches the end of the filling.
4. Next, start on the opposite side of the egg roll wrapper and fold over the two tucked in corners and the egg roll filling. Continue to roll the eggroll tightly (but not too tight) until it is rolled into a cylindar.
5. Use a basting brush to brush water on the edge of the eggroll to seal it.

6. Spray the outside of the rolled eggroll with vegetable oil and cook for 8 minutes in the air fryer on 375, turning halfway through.

Air Fryer French Toast

Servings: 4
Cooking Time: 8 minutes

Ingredients:
- 2 Eggs
- 4 Slices of bread
- 2 tbsp Heavy Whipping Cream
- 1 tsp Kosher Salt
- 1 tsp pepper
- 1 tsp Ground Cinnamon
- 1/4 cup powdered sugar

Directions:
1. Mix your egg, heavy cream, salt, pepper, and cinnamon in a mixing bowl
2. Warm a teaspoon of butter in the bottom of your heatsafe pan
3. Add the dredged pieces of bread to the pan
4. Cook for 5 minutes
5. Flip the french toast
6. Cook for an additional 3 minutes
7. Remove from the air fryer
8. Sprinkle with powdered sugar and top with berries and whipped cream (optional)

Air Fryer Ravioli (1)

Servings: 2
Cooking Time: 6 minutes

Ingredients:
- 12 frozen ravioli
- 1/2 cup buttermilk*
- 1/2 cup Italian breadcrumbs
- Also
- Marinara sauce for dipping
- Oil for spritzing

Directions:
1. Preheat air fryer to 400 degrees.

2. Place two bowls side by side. Put the buttermilk in one and breadcrumbs in the other.

3. Dip each piece of ravioli into the buttermilk then breadcrumbs, making sure to coat it as best as possible.

4. Place each breaded ravioli into the air fryer in one single layer and cook for 6-7 minutes, spritzing the tops with oil halfway through.

5. Remove the air fryer and enjoy immediately with marinara or freeze for up to 3 months.

Air Fryer Ravioli (2)

Servings: 4
Cooking Time: 10 minutes

Ingredients:
- 1 Eggs
- 1 cup bread crumbs
- 1/4 cup shredded parmesan cheese
- 1 tsp Kosher Salt
- 1/2 tsp Ground Black Pepper
- 1 tsp Dried Oregano
- Basil leaves to garnish
- 1 package Cheese Ravioli

Directions:
1. How To Make Air Fryer Ravioli (Not Frozen)
2. Scramble the eggs in a bowl
3. Mix the bread crumbs, salt, pepper, parmesan, and oregano in a bowl
4. Dip the premade ravioli in the egg mixture
5. Dip the premade ravioli in the bread crumb mixture
6. Place the ravioli in a single layer in the air fryer basket
7. Air fry the ravioli at 375F for 8 minutes
8. How To Make Frozen Toasted Ravioli
9. Place the ravioli in a single layer in the air fryer basket
10. Cook at 375F for 22 minutes, flipping half way
11. Serve with your favorite dipping sauce

Air Fryer Hard Boiled Eggs

Servings: 1
Cooking Time: 14 minutes

Ingredients:
- 4 eggs

1. **Directions:**
2. Place eggs in air fryer on tray or on top of trivet
3. Cook for 14 minutes at 250F
4. Let rest in an ice bath for 5 minutes
5. Gently crack shells
6. Carefully peel the hard shell away from the hard boiled egg under running water

Air Fried Herb and Cheese Frittata

Servings: 4
Cooking Time: 15 minutes

Ingredients:

- 4 Eggs
- 1/2 cup Half and Half
- 1/3 cup shredded sharp cheddar cheese
- 2 tablespoons Chopped Green Scallions
- 2 tablespoons Chopped Cilantro or Parsley
- 1/2 teaspoon Kosher Salt
- 1/2 teaspoon Ground Black Pepper

Directions:

1. Using a pastry brush or a silicone brush, grease a heat safe pan 6-inch pan that will fit into your air fryer basket. Be sure to grease the pan well, since eggs stick it something fierce. Alternatively, you can place a parchment paper round on the bottom of your pan.
2. In a large bowl, beat together eggs and half-and-half. Stir in all remaining ingredients.
3. Place the pan into the air fryer basket.
4. Set the air fryer to 330F for 15 minutes, or until the frittata is set and a toothpick inserted into the center emerges clean.
5. Very carefully take out the hot pan and serve your delicious frittata either hot or at room temperature.

Air Fryer Chili Cheese Toast

Servings: 1
Cooking Time: 5 minutes

Ingredients:

- 2 tablespoon Grated Parmesan Cheese
- 2 tablespoon Grated Mozzarella
- 2 teaspoon Butter
- 8 slices Serrano peppers

- 2 slices sourdough bread
- 1/2 tsp Ground Black Pepper optional

Directions:

1. In a small bowl, mix together the grated cheeses, butter and chilis. You want to make a bit of a paste with all this before you spread it on the bread, because if you don't, you will have airborne shreds of cheese flying about the air fryer.

2. Spread this paste on to the 2 slices of sourdough bread.

3. Place the slices of bread on in the air fryer basket and cook at 330F for 5 minutes, until the cheese has melted.

DESSERTS RECIPES

Keto Chocolate Chaffle Recipe

Servings: 2
Cooking Time: 8 minutes

Ingredients:
- 1/2 cup Sugar-Free Chocolate Chips
- 1/2 cup Butter
- 3 Eggs
- 1/4 cup Truvia or other sweetener
- 1 teaspoon Vanilla extract

Directions:
1. In a microwave safe bowl, melt butter and chocolate for about 1 minute. Remove and stir well. You really want to use the heat within the butter and chocolate to melt the rest of the clumps. If you microwave until it's all melted, you've overcooked the chocolate. So get a spoon and start stirring. Add 10 seconds if needed but stir well before you decide to do that.
2. In a bowl, add eggs, sweetener, and vanilla and blend until light and frothy.
3. Pour the melted butter and chocolate into the bowl in a slow stream and beat again until it is well-incorporated.
4. Pour about 1/4 of the mixture into a Dash Mini Waffle Maker, and cook for 7-8 minutes, or until crispy.
5. Should make 4 waffles, with a little batter left over.

Air Fryer German Apple Pancakes

Servings: 3
Cooking Time: 8 minutes

Ingredients:
- For the Batter
- 2 Eggs
- 1/4 cup All Purpose Flour
- 1/4 tea Baking Powder
- 1 1/2 tea Sugar Or Other Sweetener Equivalent
- 1 pinch Kosher Salt
- 1/2 cup Whole Milk
- 1/2 tea Vanilla Extract
- 1/4 tea Ground Nutmug

- 1 TBS butter melted
- For the Apples
- 1 small Granny Smith Apples Peeled, Cored, Sliced
- 1/4 cup Granulated Sugar divided
- 1/4 tea Ground Cinnamon
- 1/4 tea Ground Nutmeg
- 2 TBS Butter
- Ice Cream If Desired

Directions:

1. For the Batter
2. In a medium bowl, combine the eggs, flour, baking powder, sugar, and salt. Whisk lightly. Gradually add milk, whisking constantly. Whisk in vanilla, butter, and nutmeg. Let batter stand for 30 minutes.
3. For the Apples
4. In a small bowl, combine 2 tablespoons of sugar, cinnamon, and nutmeg. Stir until well combined; set aside.
5. Place the butter in a 6-inch round baking pan. Place the plan in the air fryer basket. Set the air fryer to 400°F for 2 minutes. When butter is melted and pan is hot, brush some of the butter up the sides of the pan.
6. Sprinkle the spiced sugar mixture over the butter. Arrange apple slices in the pan in a single layer. Sprinkle the remaining 2 tablespoons sugar over the apples.
7. Set the air fryer to 2 minutes or until the mixture bubbles.
8. Gently pour the batter mixture over the apples. Set the air fryer to 350°F and bake for 12 minutes, or until batter is golden brown around the edges and center is cooked through.
9. Serve immediately with ice cream, if desired.

Air Fryer Chocolate Chip Cookies

Servings: 18
Cooking Time: 8 minutes

Ingredients:

- 2 1/2 cups All-Purpose Flour
- 1/2 tsp Kosher Salt
- 1 tsp Baking Soda
- 1 tsp Baking Powder
- 3/4 cup softened butter
- 2 Eggs
- 3/4 cup Brown Sugar
- 2 tsp Vanilla extract
- 12 oz chocolate chips

- 1/2 cup granulated sugar

Directions:

1. Blend together softened butter, sugars, egg, and vanilla in a mixing bowl
2. In a separaget bowl, mix flour, salt, baking soda, and baking powder
3. Slowly incorporate the flour mixture into the butter and sugar mixture until well blended
4. Fold in the chocolate chips
5. Heat your air fryer to 350F
6. Place a layer of parchment paper or aluminum foil inside your air fryer basket where you will be baking your cookies
7. Place your cookie dough balls approximately 2 inches apart on top of the parchment paper
8. Gently flatten your cookie dough balls with the palm of your hand or the bottom of a glass so they resemble a cookie shape instead of a ball. They should still be about 1/2" thick
9. Cook for 6-8 minutes or until your cookies are beginning to crisp on the edges but are still gooey in the middle

Air Fryer Brownies (1)

Servings: 4
Cooking Time: 15 minutes

Ingredients:

- ¼ cup semisweet chocolate chips divided (45g)
- ¼ cup unsalted butter (57g)
- ½ cup granulated sugar (100g)
- 1 large egg
- 1 teaspoon vanilla extract
- ⅓ cup all-purpose flour (40g)
- ¼ cup Dutch-process cocoa powder (25g)
- ¼ teaspoon salt

Directions:

1. Butter the bottom and sides of a 6-inch baking pan and line the bottom with parchment paper.
2. Place the chocolate chips and the butter in a medium microwave-safe bowl. Microwave in 30-second increments, stirring between each, until the chocolate is fully melted.
3. Whisk in the sugar, egg, and vanilla until smooth. Add the flour, cocoa powder, and salt, and stir until well combined. If desired, stir an additional ¼ cup of chocolate chips into the batter. Transfer the batter to the prepared baking pan and smooth the top.
4. Preheat the air fryer to 330°F.
5. Place pan in the air fryer basket and cook until the top is crackly, the edges are set, and a toothpick inserted into the center comes out with fudge batter, about 15 minutes. (The brownies will continue to set up in the pan as they cool, but you can cook for an additional 3 to 5 minutes for a less fudgy center.)

6. Let the brownies cool completely in the pan before cutting and serving.

Air Fryer Brownies (2)

Servings: 2
Cooking Time: 30 minutes

Ingredients:
- 1/4 cup All-Purpose Flour
- 1/4 tsp Baking Powder
- 1/2 tsp Kosher Salt
- 1/2 cup Unsweetened Cocoa Powder
- 1/2 cup granulated sugar
- 1/2 cup Butter
- 1 egg
- 1/4 cup Sugar-Free Chocolate Chips

Directions:
1. Mix together dry ingredients in a large mixing bowl
2. Slowly add in eggs one at a time, mixing between each
3. Line your 7" pan with parchment paper or aluminum foil
4. Pour the batter into the prepared baking pan
5. Cook at 325F for 15-17 minutes

Air Fryer Biscuits Recipe

Servings: 8
Cooking Time: 10 minutes

Ingredients:
- 3/4 cup unbleached all-purpose flour
- 1/2 teaspoon Kosher Salt
- 1/4 teaspoon Cayenne Pepper
- 1/4 teaspoon Smoked Paprika
- 1/4 teaspoon Ground Black Pepper
- 1 dash Garlic Powder
- 1/4 cup Butter softened
- 1 cup shredded sharp cheddar cheese room temperature
- Non-Stick Cooking Spray

Directions:
1. In a food processor, combine the flour, salt, cayenne, smoked paprika, and black pepper and garlic powder,

if using. Pulse to combine.

2. Add the butter and cheese and process until the dough is smooth and has the texture of play clay. (Or, make the dough in a stand mixer fitted with the paddle attachment.

3. On a lightly floured surface, roll dough into 32 small cheese balls. Spray the air fryer basket with nonstick cooking spray. Arrange 16 drops in the air fryer basket.

4. Set the air fryer to 330°F for 10 minutes or until drops are just starting to brown. Repeat with remaining dough.

5. Cool cheese drops completely on a wire rack. Store in an airtight container.

Air Fried Phyllo Brie

Servings: 6
Cooking Time: 15 minutes

Ingredients:
- 8 sheets packaged phyllo pastry at room temperature
- 8 ounces Brie cheese
- 2 tablespoons fig jam or cranberry jelly
- 1/3 cup melted butter

Directions:
1. Place 1 sheet of phyllo pastry in a springform pan. Press the phyllo to conform to the shape of the pan. Lightly brush with some of the melted butter. I will admit we used Coconut Oil Pam but you use whatever you want.

2. Place another sheet of phyllo on top, off-setting the corners of the sheets so you have some overlap. Lightly brush with some of the melted butter or Pam. Continue in this fashion until you have used up all 8 sheets, being sure to brush or spray liberally between sheets. Make sure that you are pressing the sheets on to the sides of the pan. You are using the pan as a mold to get a perfectly rounded pastry,

3. Lightly scrape off some of the brie rind. We used a vegetable peeler to do this. Place the brie, remaining rind and all, into the center of the phyllo sheets. Spread with fig jam or cranberry jelly.

4. Carefully fold over the phyllo sheets one sheet at a time,   and brush with butter or spray with Pam. Press them down so the brie is well covered, ensuring the sheets stick together. Spray the top liberally when done.

5. Set your airfryer to 390F for 15 minutes and check after 10 minutes to ensure it is cooking evenly.

6. Once the outside is browned, the brie is melted, and it is ready to serve.

Fruit Hand Pies

Servings: 2
Cooking Time: 35 minutes

Ingredients:

- For the Crust
- 1.5 cups All-Purpose Flour
- 1/2 teaspoon Kosher Salt
- 1/4 cup shortening cup up
- 1/4 cup Butter cut up
- 1/4-1/3 cup cold water
- For the Fruit Filling
- 1 large Eggs
- 1 tablespoon Water
- 1 teaspoon coarse sugar

Directions:

1. Preheat the air fryer to 320°F.
2. On a piece of 8 1/2 x 11-inch paper, trace around a 6-inch round baking pan. Cut out the circle (this will be the pattern for cutting out the pie crusts); set aside.
3. In a medium bowl, stir together the flour and salt. Using a pastry blender, cut in the shortening and butter until pieces are pea-size. Sprinkle 1 tablespoon of the cold water over part of the flour mixture. Toss with a fork. Move the moistened pastry to the side of the bowl. Repeat with remaining flour, using 1 tablespoon of the water at a time, until everything is moist. Gather the flour mixture into a ball and knead gently only as much time as it takes to come together in a ball.
4. On a lightly floured surface, slightly flatten the pastry, then roll from the center to the edge into a 13-inch circle. Place the pattern on the pastry near one edge. Using a small, sharp knife, cut out a 6-inch circle of pastry. Repeat to make two circles. Discard dough scraps.
5. Place half of the desired Fruit Filling on half of the pastry circle, leaving a ¼-inch border. Brush the bare edge with water. Fold the empty half of the pastry over the filling. Using a fork, press around the edge of the pastry to seal it. Poke the top in a few places with a fork. Repeat with remaining filling and pastry.
6. In a small bowl, beat together the egg and water. Brush over the tops of the pies and sprinkle with the coarse sugar.
7. Place the pies in the air fryer basket and cook for 35 minutes or until pies are golden brown.
8. Cool pies on a wire rack for 20 minutes before serving.

Pumpkin Spice Bread Pudding with Maple Cream Sauce

Servings: 6
Cooking Time: 35 minutes

Ingredients:

- 3/4 cup Heavy Cream
- 1/2 cup canned pumpkin puree
- 1/3 cup Whole Milk

- 1/3 cup Sugar Or Other Sweetener Equivalent
- 1 large Eggs plus 1 yolk
- 1/8 teaspoon Kosher Salt
- 1/2 teaspoon Pumpkin Pie Spice
- 4 cups cubed (1 inch) day-old baguette or crusty country bread
- 4 tablespoons Unsalted Butter melted
- For the sauce
- 1/2 cup Heavy Cream
- 1/3 cup pure maple syrup
- 1 tablespoon Unsalted Butter
- 1/2 teaspoon vanilla extract

Directions:

1. For the Bread Pudding
2. In a medium bowl whisk together cream, pumpkin, milk, sugar, egg and yolk, salt, and pumpkin pie spice.
3. In a large bowl toss bread cubes with melted butter. Add pumpkin mixture and toss gently until everything is thoroughly combined.
4. Transfer mixture to an ungreased 6-inch round or square baking pan. Place pan in air fryer basket. Set fryer to 350°F for 35-40 minutes, or until custard is set in the middle.
5. You can also bake this in a regular oven at 375F for 30 minutes, or until custard is set in the middle.
6. For the Sauce
7. In a small saucepan heat maple syrup and butter over medium heat, stirring until butter melts. Stir in heavy cream and simmer, stirring often, until sauce has thickened, about 15 minutes.
8. Let bread pudding stand for 10 minutes before serving with warm Maple-Cream Sauce.

Air Fryer Fruit Cake

Servings: 6
Cooking Time: 30 minutes

Ingredients:
- 1 cup Dried Fruit
- 2 cups hot water
- 1 cup fine farina or rava/sooji or cream of wheat, milled fine
- 1 cup Whole Milk
- 1 cup Sugar Or Other Sweetener Equivalent
- 1/4 cup Ghee or Oil
- 1/4 cup sour cream or plain yogurt
- 1 tsp Ground Cardamom
- 1 tsp Baking Powder
- 1/2 tsp Baking Soda

Directions:

1. Soak the dried fruit in hot water and set aside to plump up.
2. Grease an 8 inch heat-safe baking pan and set aside.
3. Meanwhile, in a large mixing bowl whisk together the farina, milk, sugar, ghee, sour cream, and cardamom.
4. Set this aside for 20 minutes to allow the farina to soften and absorb some of the liquid.
5. Drain the dried fruit very well, and mix it with the batter.
6. Add the baking powder and baking soda and mix well.
7. Pour the cake mix into the greased pan and set the pan in the air fryer basket.
8. Set your air fryer to 330F for 25 minutes.
9. At the end of the cook time, insert a toothpick to check for doneness. When the toothpick emerges clean, remove the pan and let it rest for 10 minutes before unmolding the cake.

FISH AND SEAFOOD RECIPES

Air Fryer Fish Nuggets

Servings: 4
Cooking Time: 12 minutes

Ingredients:
- 1 pound Tilapia
- 1/2 cup All Purpose Flour
- 2 Eggs
- 1 cup Panko Bread Crumbs
- 1 tsp Garlic Powder
- 1 tsp Paprika
- 1/2 tsp Kosher Salt
- 1/2 tsp Black Pepper
- Olive Oil Spray

Directions:
1. Prepare the Fish. Cut the fish fillets into bite-sized pieces. Pat them dry with paper towels to help the coating stick better.
2. Set Up Breading Station. In one shallow bowl, place the flour. In a second bowl, beat the eggs. In a third bowl, combine the panko breadcrumbs, garlic powder, paprika, salt, and pepper.
3. Bread the Fish Nuggets. Dip each piece of fish first in the flour, shaking off any excess. Then dip in the beaten eggs, and finally coat thoroughly in the panko breadcrumb mixture.
4. Air Fry. Preheat the air fryer to 400°F. Spray the air fryer basket with olive oil. Place the breaded fish nuggets in a single layer in the basket, ensuring they don't touch. Lightly spray the tops with olive oil. Cook for 10-12 minutes, flipping halfway through, until the nuggets are golden brown and crispy. The internal temperature should reach 145°F.
5. Serve. Serve your fish nuggets hot, with a side of tartar sauce, lemon wedges, or your favorite dipping sauce.

Air Fryer Tilapia (1)

Servings: 4
Cooking Time: 15 minutes

Ingredients:
- 4 tilapia fillets 4-6 ounces each
- 3 tablespoons olive oil or melted butter

- ½ teaspoon paprika
- ¼ teaspoon chili powder
- ¼ teaspoon ground black pepper
- ¼ teaspoon garlic powder or granules
- ¼ teaspoon onion powder
- ½ teaspoon salt
- For Serving:
- lemon wedges

Directions:

1. Preheat your air fryer to 375°F/180°C for 5 minutes.Make the Seasoning Blend: Combine the seasoning and spices in a small bowl.
2. Pat the fillet dry and drizzle it with olive oil, then use a pastry brush or your hands to lightly coat the fish all over with the oil. Sprinkle the seasoning over both sides of the fish.
3. Line the basket with a parchment paper liner if you prefer to use one. Add the fish to the air fryer basket and air fry for 6–7 minutes making sure to flip halfway through.
4. Let the air fryer tilapia rest for 5 minutes then serve it with lemon wedges and sides of your choice.

Air Fryer Tilapia (2)

Servings: 2
Cooking Time: 10 minutes

Ingredients:
- 2 Tilapia Fillets
- 1 tsp Garlic Minced
- 1/2 tsp Salt
- 1/4 tsp Black Pepper
- 1/2 tsp Red Pepper Flakes
- Lemon Juice freshly squeezed
- Parsley for garnish
- Cooking Spray

Directions:

1. Season tilapia filets with salt, pepper, minced garlic, and red pepper flakes
2. Spray both sides of the filets with oil
3. Place the tilapia in the air fryer basket
4. Cook at 400F for 5 minutes.
5. Carefully flip the filets and cook for an additional 4-5 minutes or until it reaches an internal temperature of 145F
6. Remove the fish from the air fryer and finish with fresh lemon juice and fresh parsley

Air Fryer Honey Glazed Salmon Recipe

Servings: 4
Cooking Time: 10 minutes

Ingredients:

- 16 oz Salmon Filets
- 3 tbsp Honey
- 2 tbsp Soy Sauce
- 2 tbsp Olive Oil
- 2 tbsp Minced Garlic
- 1 tsp Ginger
- 1/2 tsp Black Pepper
- 1/2 tsp Red Pepper Flakes
- lemon or lime For Garnish
- Green Onion For Garnish

Directions:

1. Prepare the Glaze. In a small bowl, whisk together the honey, soy sauce, olive oil, minced garlic, grated ginger, ground black pepper, and red pepper flakes (if using). This delectable glaze will be the key to imparting rich flavor and a beautiful caramelization to the salmon.
2. Marinate the Salmon. Place the salmon fillets in a shallow dish or a resealable plastic bag. Pour half of the honey glaze over the salmon, reserving the other half for basting during cooking. Make sure the salmon is evenly coated with the glaze. Cover the dish or seal the bag and refrigerate for at least 30 minutes to allow the flavors to infuse into the salmon.
3. Preheat the Air Fryer. Preheat your air fryer to 400F for a few minutes to ensure it's nice and hot before cooking the salmon.
4. Air Fry the Salmon. Remove the salmon from the marinade and shake off any excess liquid. Place the salmon fillets in the air fryer basket, making sure they are not touching. Air fry the salmon for 8-10 minutes, depending on the thickness of the fillets. Baste the salmon with the reserved honey glaze halfway through the cooking time to enhance the flavor.
5. Serve and Garnish. Once the salmon is cooked to perfection, remove it from the air fryer basket and transfer it to a serving plate. Garnish with fresh lemon slices and chopped green onions for a burst of freshness and a pop of color.

Air Fryer Crab Rangoon

Servings: 24
Cooking Time: 8 minutes

Ingredients:

- 8 ounces lump crab meat
- 8 ounces cream cheese
- 2 green onions
- 1 tsp minced garlic
- 1 tsp soy sauce
- 1/2 tsp Worchestershire sauce
- 1/4 tsp Ground Ginger
- 1/4 tsp White Pepper
- 24 Wonton Wrappers
- Cooking Spray

Directions:

1. In a mixing bowl, combine the softened cream cheese, minced garlic, chopped green onions, soy sauce, Worcestershire sauce, ground ginger, and white pepper. Mix until all the ingredients are well incorporated. Gently fold in the flaked crabmeat, being careful not to break up the meat too much. The mixture should be evenly combined, with visible chunks of crabmeat throughout.
2. Place the filling in the center of the wrapper and fold it up tight using the steps provided below.
3. Preheat your air fryer to 375F for about 5 minutes.Lightly spray the air fryer basket with non-stick cooking spray to prevent sticking.Arrange the crab rangoon in a single layer in the air fryer basket, making sure they are not touching each other.Lightly spray the crab rangoon with non-stick cooking spray.Place the basket in the air fryer and cook for 8-10 minutes or until the crab rangoon are golden brown and crispy. Flip them halfway through the cooking time for even browning.
4. Allow the crab rangoon to cool for a few minutes before serving, as the filling can be extremely hot. Serve the Crab Rangoon on a platter, alongside a dipping sauce of your choice.

Air Fryer Coconut Shrimp (5)

Servings: 4
Cooking Time: 10 minutes

Ingredients:
- 1 pound Raw Shrimp
- 1 cup Unsweetened Shredded Coconut
- 2 eggs
- 1/2 cup all purpose flour
- 1 tsp garlic powder
- 1/2 tsp paprika
- 1/2 tsp salt
- 1/2 tsp black pepper

Directions:

1. Preheat your air fryer. Set your air fryer to 400F and let it preheat for a few minutes while you prepare

the shrimp.

2. Prepare the coating station. In three separate shallow bowls, set up your coating station. In the first bowl, place the flour. In the second bowl, beat the eggs with a fork until well combined. In the third bowl, combine the shredded coconut, garlic powder, paprika, salt, and black pepper.

3. Coat the shrimp. Take a shrimp and dip it into the flour, ensuring it's evenly coated. Shake off any excess flour. Then dip it into the beaten eggs, allowing any excess to drip off. Finally, coat the shrimp with the coconut mixture, pressing gently to adhere to the coconut flakes. Place the coated shrimp on a plate or tray, and repeat the process with the remaining shrimp.

4. Air frying the shrimp. Lightly spray the air fryer basket with cooking spray to prevent sticking. Arrange the coconut-coated shrimp in a single layer, leaving space between them for proper air circulation. Depending on the size of your air fryer, you may need to cook the shrimp in batches.

5. Air frying time. Cook the shrimp in the preheated air fryer for approximately 8-10 minutes, flipping them halfway through the cooking time. Keep a close eye on the shrimp to ensure they don't overcook or burn. The shrimp should turn golden brown and become crispy.

6. Serve and enjoy. Once the shrimp are cooked to perfection, remove them from the air fryer and transfer them to a serving platter. Garnish with some fresh herbs or a sprinkle of toasted coconut for an extra touch of tropical flair. Serve them hot with your favorite dipping sauce.

Air Fried Salt and Pepper Shrimp

Servings: 4
Cooking Time: 10 minutes

Ingredients:
- 2 teaspoons Whole Black Peppercorns ground
- 2 teaspoons Sichuan peppercorns ground
- 1 teaspoon Kosher Salt
- 1 teaspoon Sugar Or Other Sweetener Equivalent
- 1 pound Shrimp 21-25 per pound
- 3 tablespoons Rice Flour
- 2 tablespoons Oil

Directions:
1. Heat a saucepan on medium heat and roast the black peppercorns and sichuan peppercorns together for 1-2 minutes until you can smell the aroma from the peppercorns. Allow them to cool.
2. Add salt and sugar, and using a mortar and pestle, crush the spices together to form a coarse powder.
3. Place shrimp in a large bowl. Add the spices, rice flour and oil, and mix well until the shrimp are well-coated.
4. Place the shrimp in the airfryer basket, trying to keep them in as flat a layer as possible. You may want to use a rack, and place half the shrimp in the basket and the other half on the rack.
5. Spray well with additional oil.

6. Set the air fryer to 325F and cook for 8-10 minutes, tossing halfway through.

Air Fryer Fish in Parchment paper

Servings: 2
Cooking Time: 15 minutes

Ingredients:
- 2 5-oz Cod Fillets thawed
- 1/2 cup julienned carrots
- 1/2 cup julienned fennel bulbs or 1/4 cup julienned celery
- 1/2 cup thinly sliced red peppers
- 2 sprigs tarragon or 1/2 teaspoon dried tarragon
- 2 pats melted butter
- 1 tablespoon Lemon Juice
- 1 tablespoon Kosher Salt divided
- 1/2 teaspoon Ground Black Pepper
- 1 tablespoon Oil

Directions:
1. In a medium bowl combine melted butter, tarragon, 1/2 teaspoon salt, and lemon juice. Mix well until you get a creamy sauce. Add the julienned vegetable and mix well. Set aside.
2. Cut two squares of parchment large enough o hold the fish and vegetables.
3. Spray the fish fillets with oil and apply salt and pepper to both sides of the fillets.
4. Lay one filet down on each parchment square. Top each fillet with half the vegetables. Pour any remaining sauce over the vegetables.
5. Fold over the parchment paper and crimp the sides to hold fish, veggies and sauce securely inside the packet. Place the packets inside the airfryer basket.
6. Set your airfryer to 350F for 15 minutes. Remove each packet to a plate and open just before serving.

Air Fryer Cajun Shrimp

Servings: 4
Cooking Time: 10 minutes

Ingredients:
- FOR THE SAUCE
- 1/2 cup Mayonnaise
- 1 Garlic Cloves minced
- 2 teaspoons Lemon Juice
- 2 tablespoons creole mustard

- 1/2 teaspoon hot pepper sauce
- 1 tablespoon sweet pickle relish
- 1 Chopped Green Scallions chopped
- 1/2 teaspoons Worcestershire Sauce
- 1/4 teaspoon Smoked Paprika
- 1/4 teaspoon Kosher Salt
- FOR THE SHRIMP
- 1/2 cup Half and Half
- 1 Eggs
- 1 tablespoon Cajun Seasoning without salt, divided
- 1 1/2 cups finely ground cornmeal
- 1 pound Raw Shrimp large, peeled and deveined, 21-25 count
- Kosher Salt to taste
- Ground Black Pepper to taste
- Vegetable

Directions:

1. FOR THE SAUCE
2. In a small bowl combine the mayonnaise, garlic, mustard, hot pepper sauce, relish, green onion, Worcestershire sauce, paprika, and salt. Stir until well combined. Cover and chill until serving time.
3. FOR THE SHRIMP
4. In a large bowl, whisk together the half and half, egg, and 1 teaspoon of the Cajun seasoning. Add the shrimp and toss gently to combine. Refrigerate for at least 15 minutes or up to 1 hour.
5. Meanwhile, in a shallow dish, whisk together the cornmeal, remaining 2 teaspoons Cajun seasoning, and salt and pepper to taste.
6. Spray the air-fryer basket with vegetable oil spray. Dredge the shrimp in the cornmeal mixture until well-coated. Shake off any excess and arrange in a single layer the air-fryer basket. Spray shrimp with vegetable oil spray.
7. Set the air fryer to 350°F for 10 minutes, carefully turning and spraying the shrimp with vegetable oil spray halfway through the cooking time.
8. Serve the shrimp with the sauce.

Keto Shrimp Scampi

Servings: 4
Cooking Time: 10 minutes

Ingredients:
- 4 tablespoons Butter
- 1 tablespoon Lemon Juice
- 1 tablespoon Minced Garlic

- 2 teaspoons Red Pepper Flakes
- 1 tablespoon chopped chives or 1 teaspoon dried chives
- 1 tablespoon chopped fresh basil or 1 teaspoon dried basil
- 2 tablespoons Chicken Stock (or white wine)
- 1 lb Raw Shrimp (21-25 count)

Directions:

1. Turn your air fryer to 330F. Place a 6 x 3 metal pan in it and allow it to start heating while you gather your ingredients.
2. Place the butter, garlic, and red pepper flakes into the hot 6-inch pan.
3. Allow it to cook for 2 minutes, stirring once, until the butter has melted. Do not skip this step. This is what infuses garlic into the butter, which is what makes it all taste so good.
4. Open the air fryer, add butter, lemon juice,, minced garlic, red pepper flakes, chives, basil, chicken stock, and shrimp to the pan in the order listed, stirring gently.
5. Allow shrimp to cook for 5 minutes, stirring once. At this point, the butter should be well-melted and liquid, bathing the shrimp in spiced goodness.
6. Mix very well, remove the 6-inch pan using silicone mitts, and let it rest for 1 minute on the counter. You're doing this so that you let the shrimp cook in the residual heat, rather than letting it accidentally overcook and get rubbery.
7. Stir at the end of the minute. The shrimp should be well-cooked at this point.
8. Sprinkle additional fresh basil leaves and enjoy.

Air Fryer Salmon Patties

Servings: 2
Cooking Time: 15 minutes

Ingredients:
- 2 5 ounce pouches Salmon Packets wild-caught
- 1 large Eggs beaten
- 4 tablespoons Panko
- 1 Chopped Green Scallions finely chopped, white and light green parts
- 1 teaspoon Dried Dill
- 1/2 teaspoon Kosher Salt
- 1/2 teaspoon Ground Black Pepper
- Cooking Oil Spray
- Lemon wedges

Directions:
1. In a large bowl, combine the salmon, egg, bread crumbs, scallion, dillweed, and salt and black pepper to taste. Gently mix until well-combined. Form into 4 patties.
2. Spray the air fryer basket with cooking spray. Lightly mist both sides of the patties with cooking spray.

3. Arrange the patties in the air fryer basket. Set the air fryer to 400°F for 15 minutes. Halfway through the cooking time, turn the patties and spray both sides with more vegetable oil spray. When done, patties should be golden-brown and crisp.

4. Serve croquettes hot with lemon wedges.

Air Fryer Shrimp Fried Rice

Servings: 4
Cooking Time: 25 minutes

Ingredients:
- For the Shrimp
- 1 pound Shrimp peeled and deveined
- 1/4 teaspoon pepper
- 1 teaspoon Cornstarch
- For the Rice
- 2 cups Cooked Rice
- 1 cup Frozen Peas and Carrots thawed
- 1/4 cup Chopped Green Scallions chopped
- 3 tablespoon sesame oil
- 1 tablespoon soy sauce
- 1/2 teaspoon Kosher Salt
- 1 teaspoon pepper
- For the Eggs
- 2 large Eggs beaten
- 1/4 teaspoon Kosher Salt
- 1/4 teaspoon pepper

Directions:
1. Combine shrimp with salt and cornstarch. Set aside.
2. In a 6 x 3 heatproof pan, mix together the rice, vegetables, onions, sesame oil, salt, and pepper.
3. Cook in the Air Fryer at 350° for 15 minutes. Toss the rice halfway through cook time.
4. Place shrimp on top of rice and cook in Air Fryer at 350° for 5 minutes.
5. While the shrimp cooks beat the eggs with salt and pepper. Pour the eggs on top of the shrimp and rice mixture and cook another 5 minutes at 350°.
6. Stir the eggs into the shrimp and rice and serve.

Air Fryer Scallops

Servings: 2
Cooking Time: 10 minutes

Ingredients:
- 3/4 cup Heavy Whipping Cream
- 1 tablespoon Tomato Paste
- 1 tablespoon chopped fresh basil
- 1 teaspoon Minced Garlic
- 1/2 teaspoon Kosher Salt
- 1/2 teaspoon Ground Black Pepper
- 1 12 oz Frozen Spinach thawed and drained
- 8 jumbo sea scallops
- Cooking Oil Spray
- additional salt and pepper to season scallops

Directions:
1. Spray a 7-inch heatproof pan, and place the spinach in an even layer at the bottom.
2. Spray both sides of the scallops with vegetable oil, sprinkle a little more salt and pepper on them, and place scallops in the pan on top of the spinach.
3. In a small bowl, mix together the cream, tomato paste, basil, garlic, salt and pepper and pour over the spinach and scallops.
4. Set the airfryer to 350F for 10 minutes until the scallops are cooked through to an internal temperature of 135F and the sauce is hot and bubbling. Serve immediately.

Bang Bang Shrimp

Servings: 4
Cooking Time: 30 minutes

Ingredients:
- For the Shrimp
- 1 pound Raw Shrimp peeled and deveined
- 2 tablespoons cornstarch or rice flour
- 1/2 teaspoon Kosher Salt
- Cooking Oil Spray
- For the Sauce
- 1/2 cup mayonnaise
- 1/4 cup Thai sweet chili sauce
- 2-4 tablespoons Sriracha Sauce
- 1 teaspoon Minced Garlic

Directions:
1. For the sauce: In a small bowl, mix together the mayonnaise, Thai sweet chili sauce, sriracha sauce and garlic.

2. For the shrimp: In a medium bowl or a plastic ziptop bag, toss together the shrimp, cornstarch and salt until the shrimp is coated with the cornstarch or rice flour.

3. Place the shrimp in the air fryer basket, trying to keep them in as flat a layer as possible. You may want to use a rack, and place half the shrimp in the basket and the other half on the rack.

4. Spray well with additional oil.

5. Set the air fryer to 330F and cook for 10 minutes, tossing halfway through and spraying with additional oil.

6. Remove the shrimp and toss into the bowl with the half sauce. Set the other half of the sauce aside to serve as a dipping sauce.

7. Put the shrimp back into the air fryer basket. Set the air fryer to 330F for 4-5 minutes until the sauce has formed a glaze. Serve with the sauce.

OTHER FAVORITE AIR FRYER RECIPES

Reheat Fried Pickles In Air Fryer

Servings: 2
Cooking Time: 6 minutes

Ingredients:
- 500 g Leftover Dill Pickle Chips
- Extra Virgin Olive Oil Spray

Directions:
1. Place leftover dill pickle chips on a single layer in the air fryer basket.
2. Then spray the tops of pickle chips with olive oil spray.
3. Reheat fried pickles in the air fryer at 200c/400f for 6 minutes.

Frozen Pie In Air Fryer

Servings: 4
Cooking Time: 20 minutes

Ingredients:
- 4 Frozen Pies
- Egg Wash optional

Directions:
1. Remove the frozen pies from the packaging and place into the air fryer basket. Spread them out, so that they are side by side and none are on top of each other. Or if using a Air Fryer (like we are) you can usually fit 2 in each drawer.
2. Cook the frozen pies in the air fryer for 15 minutes at 180c/360f.
3. Then brush the tops of the pies with egg wash. At this point they will be almost cooked, they just need that last few minutes. Then cook for another 5 minutes at the same temperature.

Pukka Pie In Air Fryer

Servings: 2
Cooking Time: 15 minutes

Ingredients:
- 2 Frozen Pukka Pies
- Egg Wash optional

Directions:

1. Remove the frozen pukka pies from the packaging and place into the air fryer basket. Spread them out, so that they are side by side and none are on top of each other.
2. Cook the pukka pies in the air fryer for 15 minutes at 180c/360f or until the pie is piping hot in the centre. If cooking the pukka pies from chilled, reduce the cook time to 12 minutes.
3. If cooking pies in the Air Fryer – you can do 1-2 in each drawer and then use the match feature to make setting the time and temperature quicker.
4. Optional – 3 minutes before the end of the cooking time, brush the tops of the pies with egg wash.

Air Fryer Curry

Servings: 4
Cooking Time: 35 minutes

Ingredients:
- 2 Medium Sweet Potatoes
- 400 g Chickpeas
- 1 Tbsp Extra Virgin Olive Oil
- 1 Tsp Dried Coriander/Cilantro
- ¼ Tsp Mild Curry Powder
- ¼ Tsp Ground Turmeric
- 1 ¼ Tsp Garam Masala
- Salt & Pepper
- For The Curry Sauce
- 4 Frozen Spinach Blocks
- 400 g Coconut Milk
- 240 ml Passata
- 4 Tsp Tikka Paste
- 2 Tsp Ginger Puree
- 2 Tsp Dried Coriander/Cilantro
- 1 Tsp Ground Cumin

Directions:

1. Peel and dice the sweet potato into small cubes. Place into a mixing bowl with a teaspoon of coriander, a generous seasoning of salt and pepper and the olive oil.
2. Mix well with your hands and place in the air fryer and spread out for an even cook. Air fry, the sweet potatoes for 20 minutes at 180c/360f or until fork tender.
3. Add the chickpeas and ¼ tsp of garam masala. Shake the air fryer or mix with a spatula for an even coating. Air fry for another 5 minutes at the same temperature.
4. In the meantime, prepare your sauce ingredients. Microwave the spinach for 3 minutes on full power if not thawed already, then use your hands to squeeze out the excess moisture.

5. Add all the sauce ingredients with the chickpeas and sweet potatoes into a container, or directly in the bottom of the Air Fryer and mix well.
6. Air fry the curry for 10 minutes at 180c/360f or until piping hot and reduced.
7. When it is ready it will have a curry colour to it and the sweet potato will be a little crispy on touch.

Air Fryer Pasta Bake

Servings: 4
Cooking Time: 8 minutes

Ingredients:
- Instant Pot Pasta
- 400 g Bolognese Sauce
- 115 g grated cheddar cheese
- 2 Tsp dried oregano
- Salt & Pepper
- Choose one of the following
- 500 g Air fryer ground beef
- 500 g Air fryer sausages
- 500 g Air fryer frozen meatballs

Directions:
1. If making your air fryer pasta bake with sausages, cook the sausages first, for 8-12 minutes at 180c/360f depending on your preferred doneness and then chop into chunks.
2. Or if air frying pasta with meatballs, you can cook them fresh or from frozen and air fry for about 10 minutes at the same temperature.
3. Place the pasta into a bowl, or your container (whatever is easiest for you) and then add the Bolognese sauce, your chosen add in and mix well with a wooden spoon.
4. Transfer to the cooking container (if you have not mixed in it) and then fully coat with grated cheese. Air fry for 8 minutes at 180c/360f or until the cheese is melted and the pasta bake is heated through.
5. Then when the air fryer beeps your pasta in the air fryer will be coated with perfectly melted cheese and ready for serving.

Air Fryer Easter Rocky Road

Servings: 9
Cooking Time: 5 minutes

Ingredients:
- 100 g Unsalted Butter
- 300 g Chocolate Egg broken into bits

- 2 Tbsp Golden Syrup
- 4 Plain Digestives/Graham Crackers
- 180 g Mini Eggs
- 100 g Mini Marshmallows
- For Decorating
- 1 Crème Eggs
- 1 Caramel Eggs
- 60 g Mini Eggs
- 3 Chocolate Rabbits
- 2 Mini Chocolate Rabbits

Directions:

1. Place the chocolate egg (broken into pieces), butter (in chunks) and golden syrup into an air fryer friendly container such as silicone. Air fry at 120c/250f for 5 minutes to melt the butter and the chocolate.
2. When the air fryer beeps, give it a good stir.
3. In the meantime, in a bowl add the mini eggs, and use the top of a rolling pin to crush it into tiny pieces, also add the biscuits and the marshmallows and stir. We recommend a few mini eggs that are whole for some texture and prettiness.
4. Add the melted chocolate mixture to the broken bits and give it a good stir. Then transfer it back to your silicone pan. Then decorate the top with favourite leftover chocolate. We included the kids chocolate bunnies, more mini eggs and sliced crème eggs and sliced caramel eggs.
5. Allow to chill in the fridge for a couple of hours and then slice into 9 pieces before serving.

Puff Pastry Pizza In Air Fryer

Servings: 2
Cooking Time: 8 minutes

Ingredients:
- For the tomato sauce
- 200 g finely chopped tinned tomatoes
- 2 Tsp tomato puree
- 1 Tsp garlic puree
- 1 Tsp dried basil
- 250 g puff pastry
- 175 g cherry tomatoes
- 225 g grated cheddar cheese
- extra cheese for stuffing 8 cheese sticks
- 2 Tsp dried oregano
- Salt & Pepper

Directions:

1. On a floured worktop with a floured rolling pin, roll out the pastry into a rectangle or a similar shape that fits your size of air fryer.

2. Optional – if you would like to create a stuffed crust, roll the pizza slightly longer at the sides, add sticks of cheese, then fold them over, so that they are hidden. You can do this to two sides of the pizza, or all four if you prefer.

3. Next mix in a small bowl the tomato sauce ingredients and brush over the pizza, leaving a 1 cm gap around the edges.

4. Finish with a topping of your pizza with your favourite toppings. I sprinkled with plenty of grated cheese, halved cherry tomatoes and you can also add a sprinkle of your favourite seasoning, then a generous sprinkling of salt and pepper.

5. Then place the pizza into the air fryer (or you might find it easier to do this before adding the toppings like I do) and air fry at 180c/360f for 8 minutes or until cooked to your preferred doneness.

Crustless Quiche In Air Fryer

Servings: 6
Cooking Time: 30 minutes

Ingredients:
- 125 g Self Raising Flour
- 5 Large Eggs
- 120 ml Whole Milk
- 1 Medium Tomato
- 1 Medium Red Onion
- 4 slices ham chopped into chunks
- 85 g Grated Cheddar Cheese
- 2 Tsp Mixed Herbs
- 2 Tsp Dried Oregano
- Salt & Pepper

Directions:
1. Crack the eggs into a mixing jug and add the milk and mix well with a fork to make a quiche batter. Then stir in your seasonings.

2. Add the remaining filling ingredients and continue to mix.

3. Add in the flour and stir.

4. Then give the mixture one last mix before pouring it into your pie dish. Though as you do scrape the edges for any of the batter that has not being poured in.

5. Place the quiche into the air fryer basket, set the temperature to 180c/360f and air fry for 20 minutes. Reduce the temperature to 160c/320f and cook for another 10 minutes or until a cocktail stick or toothpick comes out clean.

Reheat Dominos In Air Fryer

Servings: 2

Cooking Time: 4 minutes

Ingredients:
- 4 Leftover pizza
- 200 g Leftover Dominos appetisers
- 100 g Leftover nachos

Directions:
1. Spread them out in the air fryer basket and you can do a mix of what you have leftover. We did hot wings, chicken strips, potato wedges and dough balls. Cook at 160c/320f for 4 minutes.
2. We prefer these with extra cheese, so we add them to a layer of parchment paper/baking paper, and then add extra cheese. We cook them at 160c/320f for 3 minutes.
3. Dominos Pizza. Pizza is much quicker for a reheat. Though you might need to cook on a diagonal for bigger slices. Cook at 160c/320f for 3 minutes.
4. Then serve everything together on a platter and tuck in.

Reheat Burger In Air Fryer

Servings: 2

Cooking Time: 10 minutes

Ingredients:
- 2 leftover hamburgers or cheeseburgers

Directions:
1. Unwrap your leftover burger and put to one side the packaging, salad garnish that you don't want to warm up and the burger bun.
2. If the burger comes in foil, you can reheat it in the foil to save on washing up and to avoid a dirty air fryer. Then place the burgers in the air fryer and reheat for 10 minutes at 160c/320f.
3. However, if you would like a layer of melted cheese and to create the best cheeseburger, halfway through the cook time add some melted cheese.
4. Then serve your burger with the salad items, burger bun and any extra sauces you wanted to add back in.

Reheat Pizza

Servings: 2

Cooking Time: 2 minutes

Ingredients:

- 4 Slices Leftover Pizza

Directions:

1. Place up to two slices of leftover pizza into your Air Fryer basket and then place the basket into the Air Fryer main cooking pot. Place the lid down on the Air Fryer.
2. Set the temperature to 160c/320f and the time to 2 minutes on either air crisp or bake.
3. When the Air Fryer beeps serve your pizza with your favourite pizza sauces.
4. If you have lots of pizza, reheat the pizza in batches of two at a time and you can also do your leftover pizza sides.

Crimpit In Air Fryer

Servings: 2
Cooking Time: 6 minutes

Ingredients:

- 2 Weight Watchers Wraps
- 1/4 can Baked Beans
- 2 Tbsp Grated Cheddar Cheese
- 1 Egg Beaten

Directions:

1. Place your wrap over the bottom of the Crimpit and then make sure its in the right position to fill and for the top to pressed down on top. Add your filling to the Crimpit, making sure you don't overfill it.
2. Fold the wrap over to cover the top of the Crimpit.
3. Press down to create the Crimpit look and then once fully pressed down use scissors to trim off any overhang.
4. Rinse and repeat until you have done all your Crimpits.
5. Add egg wash to the tops of the Crimpits with a pastry brush.
6. Add the Crimpits into the air fryer basket. You will be able to fit four of the sandwich thins or one of the Crimpit wrap recipes.
7. Air fry Crimpits for 6 minutes at 180c/360f for the sandwich thins or 200c/400f for a Crimpit wrap.

Haggis In Air Fryer

Servings: 7
Cooking Time: 10 minutes

Ingredients:

- 7 Slices Haggis

Directions:

1. If cooking air fryer haggis slices, remove the packaging which will be easy to slip off the slices of the haggis.

2. Place the haggis slices into the air fryer basket and spread them out.
3. Air fry the haggis for 10 minutes at 180c/360f or until piping hot in the centre.
4. If the haggis is frozen it is okay to add the haggis to the air fryer whilst still stuck together. Simply add the haggis as a whole or partly whole tube and start with 8 minutes at 160c/320f, then separate and then air fry for a further 8 minutes at 180c/360f.
5. Or if cooking your haggis in its tube, place the tube into a silicone container that is of a similar size so it wont roll about too much. Then air fry for 15 minutes at 180c/360f.

Air Fryer Mince Pies

Servings: 6
Cooking Time: 12 minutes

Ingredients:
- 500 g Batch Air Fryer Pie Crust/Shortcrust Pastry
- 1/3 Jar Mincemeat
- 1 Small Egg Beaten
- 1 Tbsp Icing Sugar

Directions:
1. Let's air fry mince pies. Start by making your pastry (follow our air fryer pie crust recipe) and then flour your rolling pin and pastry and roll out. Or alternatively roll out puff pastry. Next use a round cookie cutter and cut out 6 round circles of the pastry.
2. Then gently place a round inside each of your pudding tins and push down so that you have plenty of space for your mincemeat.
3. Then using a teaspoon add two heaped teaspoons of the mincemeat into each of the pies.
4. This is how the mincemeat should look in your pastry as you don't want to add too much.
5. Next roll out the leftover pastry and cut using a heart cutter or star cutter and make 6 of them ready to go over the mincemeat.
6. Then place a heart over each of the mince pies. Followed by brushing the hearts with egg wash to help with the golden mince pie colour.
7. Place the pudding tins loaded with mince pies into the air fryer basket and air fry for 12 minutes at 180c/360f or until the pastry is cooked and the mincemeat is heated through.
8. Then allow to cool before removing the mince pies from the pudding tins.
9. For a final touch sprinkle the tops of the mince pies with icing sugar/confectioners sugar.

Air Fryer Camembert

Servings: 4
Cooking Time: 10 minutes

Ingredients:
- 1 Camembert Round
- Bread/Biscuits for serving

Directions:
1. Let's air fry camembert. Remove the packaging from the camembert and then turn the camembert over so that its bottom is now its top and it is sat in its cardboard container.
2. Then slice the top of the camembert until you have 4 lines of slices and then do the same again in the other direction.
3. Brush with your marmalade or alternatively brush with olive oil.
4. Place the camembert into the air fryer basket still in its box and air fry for 10 minutes at 180c/360f or 12 minutes if you prefer it much runnier. Check when the air fryer beeps if it is melted enough and adjust if needed.
5. Then serve the camembert with bread, biscuits, or a mixture.

Air Fryer 3 Bird Roast

Servings: 4
Cooking Time: 1 hour

Ingredients:
- 1.5 kg Turducken
- 8 Medium Potatoes
- 8 Medium Carrots
- 1 Tbsp Extra Virgin Olive Oil
- 1 Tbsp Mixed Herbs
- 2 Tsp Parsley
- Salt & Pepper

Directions:
1. Place your turducken into the air fryer basket, aiming for the middle. Air fry for 15 minutes at 180c/360f.
2. In the meantime, peel your potatoes and carrots. Chop the potatoes into quarters and then the carrots into chunks. Or you can cut the carrots into strips like you would for honey glazed carrots. Place them into a bowl and mix with oil and seasonings with your hands until well mixed.
3. When the air fryer beeps add the potatoes and carrots around the turducken filling in any spaces. Air fry for another 25 minutes at the same temperature.
4. Turn over the turducken with tongs and also shake the air fryer basket to move about the potatoes and carrots. Air fry for another 15 minutes at the same temperature.
5. Remove the turducken and allow it to rest and then air fry the potatoes and carrots for a final 5 minutes at 200c/400f to make them crispier or serve as is.

Manufactured by Amazon.ca
Bolton, ON